Rideshare Driver Secrets and Tips

Getting More Money While Driving For Uber and Lyft

By
John C. Ardussi
"The Celeb Driver"

Edited by Jenn McKee

Rideshare Driver Secrets and Tips: Getting More Money While Driving For Uber and Lyft

Cover Image: Andrey Armyagov © 123RF.com

Disclaimer

The information presented herein represents the knowledge and views based on experiences, conversations and research done by the author up until the date of publication. While the author has made his best effort to make sure the information is accurate, they make no warranties with respect to the accuracy or completeness of the contents and specifically disclaim any implied warranties.

The author shall not be liable for any loss or profit or any commercial damages. The advice and opinions contained in this book may not be suitable for your situation. This book is for informational purposes only and should not take the place of seeking professional help. For legal advice you should work with a lawyer and for financial advice, including taxes, you should work with an accountant.

Due to the rate at which data and facts are changing in this new industry, at some point this book is likely to have old information and advice that is no longer accurate. The author reserves the right to update the data and his reflections based on new information as he deems is warranted and prudent. While every attempt has been made to verify information in this book, the author does not assume any responsibility for errors, inaccuracies, or omissions.

Medieval Curse

If anyone steals or copies unlawfully from this book, may they be locked in a room with 100 angry clowns, forced to attend a Tijuana donkey show, and suffer a frighteningly unspecific pumpkin carving accident. Amen.

Dedication

This book is dedicated to my grandfather, whose calculator watch was a far weightier object than anyone should ever wear regularly; and to my father, who often brought home calculators that were programmable and used Reverse Polish Notation. I was well prepared for the coming digital revolution and all the places it has spread.

This book is also dedicated to all the crazy, fearless, funny, smart, and skilled drivers who challenged me every day while writing this book to tell the truth so that the people would know. It's important to them that the real word gets out that while driving is tough, and drivers have to work long hours for everything they get, there is no other job they would rather be doing right now. It's the job they love to hate (always with a smile).

Contents

"It's not what we don't know that hurts; it's what we know that ain't so." - *Will Rogers*

Introduction

Are you a potential new driver, looking for what to expect if you sign up for that first drive? Or are you an active driver looking for ways to improve your return on your time and investments? Either way, you've come to the right place. In this guide, I try to cover as much as I can: from your first interactions with Uber and Lyft, all the way until you file your taxes. Plus, you will find tools for maximizing your productivity at every stage.

How did I become a driver? I work from home and we were a one car family. So my wife takes the car to work leaving me to wait until she got home to go out. We discussed getting another car and she said if we did, the car would have to earn money to make sure we could pay all the added costs. Which led me too rideshare driving.

I'm a computer game developer and have been doing this work professionally for 24 years now. One thing you quickly come to understand when you play games is that winning is key, and to win, you have to know your goals. Once you have your goals listed, it's much easier to make decisions that will help you achieve them.

Sometimes your goals show you that one path is a sure loser and that's when you try a different route. The reality is that on some days, you can't win no matter how hard you try. There may simply be no path to winning that day. By having a plan, though, you can generally make your bad days better and your good days great.

One thing to keep in mind is that while there's usually a better answer that applies to most people, the best answer for you is the one that applies to your situation. For instance, most people will benefit from owning an older car with no car payments versus leasing a newer one. However, you may have a Cousin Vinny who is a Lexus dealer and can get you a bargain on a "special" car lease that you split with Rocco. Perhaps it's a lease with free unlimited mileage, thereby solving the major flaw that makes most leases a bad idea. The downside, though, is that Rocco gets it at night and you get it all day. Only you know whether that tradeoff is likely to work for you. So while I suggest the best general case answers to common questions in this guide, you should keep in mind that you must always consider your own personal circumstances.

This book will also teach you how to potentially steer people who are already paying you for one service to support you in additional ways. Plus, you'll find tips on how to get paid for nothing more than being yourself. (Kim

Kardashian, eat your heart out!)

You get all this for about the price of your morning coffee and muffin. When they said you have to spend money to make money, this book is exactly what they were talking about.

Yes, much of this information can be unearthed by searching the Internet, reading other books, watching videos, or asking questions on forums, but I have created this guide so you don't have to invest all that time. Plus, I've added knowledge I've gotten from my experiences and included strategies that have worked for me. What follows is a treasure chest of tools and behaviors that will help you be better at doing things you're going to do anyway.

My goal is to see you succeed. So sit back, grab your favorite refreshment, and read on!

Understanding Uber and Lyft

Launched in San Francisco in 2009 as UberCab, Uber has grown so fast, and received such large investments, that it's estimated to now have over 1,000,000 drivers in over 500 cities and over 70 countries around the world.

In 2012, Lyft launched as a service of Zimride, a ridesharing company started in 2007. Zimride focused on carpooling for longer trips. Lyft is an on-demand ridesharing with likely over 500,000 drivers in over 400 cities in the USA.

Understanding who you are working for and their goals will ultimately help you achieve your own.

What is Ridesharing?

Ridesharing is an evolving, on-demand car service technology platform. Passengers can use the Uber and Lyft apps on their phones to call for a driver to pick them up on the nearest road and take them to any spot to get dropped off. The core of the business is client/server location-based software, where the client software for riders and drivers runs on phones and tablets. Through servers, passengers and drivers are linked so they can find each other.

Drivers can easily join Uber's and/or Lyft's system. It usually involves significantly less paperwork, government regulations and licenses than those required for driving a taxi or limousine. Drivers are independent contractors and need to supply their own car and pay all their own taxes. Built into the system is the ability to set their own hours and drive as little or as much as they want. This flexibility helps make it more likely that drivers can meet their goals.

The CEO of Uber often talks about how driver flexibility is a goal for the company. You are not taking advantage of them by playing the game your way. If you want to drive at odd hours, the rideshare companies don't care. So enjoy!

Understanding the Companies' Goals

Of course, companies need to make money to stay open. That means they need to bring in more money than they spend. Currently, both Uber and Lyft are reportedly losing large amounts of money (Bloomberg estimates the 2016 losses for Uber at $3.8 billion), and you should remember this while setting your expectations of how they will treat drivers in the future. The amount of money that drivers make going forward is not likely to go up, as they and the companies both squeeze each other to see who explodes first.

Setting Your Goals

I know it's a little Zen to start out this early with what your goals are in a "How To" manual, but understanding the priorities of why you are doing something will help you answer most questions quickly. For instance, if one of your goals is weight loss, having a "go-to spot" to wait for rideshare pings at a Krispy Kreme is a bad idea. I'm just saying.

Almost everyone who's working as a driver is doing it for the money. (If you don't need the money, send it to me, and I'll make sure it gets to the Human Fund, a lá "Seinfeld.") For this reason, money will factor into many of the decisions you'll make.

Must-Do Goals

Your top goal should be to keep your driver rating high. Why? If your driver rating drops too low, your company can drop you as a driver. (I have heard the number 4.6 bounced around but I have not read anything official about that.) If after 100 rides or more your rating drops below a 4.8, raising it should be a priority.

For me, making a specific amount of money is a must-do goal. I promised my wife that if she let me get a new car, I would cover all the costs every month by driving. That amount is about $850/month, including the car payment, gas, insurance, and any little items I might pick up for the passengers, like water. Now that is not hard, but it has to be under the heading "must-do," or I might get lazy about it and end up having to play catch up later.

To keep yourself on track, maintain a to-do list of things you must do to keep your driver rating up, keep your car in good working condition, etc. I know it seems silly to list "change oil" when that's 5000 miles in the future, but when you are driving 200 miles a day on average, 5000 miles might be as little as 5-6 weeks away. You're a busy person, so make a list, and you'll be less likely to forget to properly service your money machine. (And by money machine I mean ... your car. You are much less useful without it.)

Finally, you need to document all your mileage and expenses. This will save you thousands of dollars later and help you avoid what will be a huge task if you wait until next year to start. If you close out each day, week and month, your taxes should be easy.

Life Goals

You should also step back and look at the big picture to consider, and list, what I call "life goals." Brainstorm what those are and consider how your driving decisions affect them. Here is a list I've compiled for myself.

For me, writing is important. So after a run, I might wait a little bit and jot down my thoughts before going back online to work.

I want to make training videos and set up a website. I want to answer emails and comments on the videos. I want to be one of the go-to people for ridesharing information.

I want to get out of the house more. My doctor actually said that was important for my health, and that I sit too much in front of my computer. I think that makes it a "must do."

I want to have enough time to work on my video games at home full time.

Make sure to list every goal, and if it is a "must do," list it properly.

Now What?

Once you have all your goals listed, sort them by priority, with the most important one at the top. Start there, and write down what you need to do to make each goal happen, and define what it will take to meet these goals and "win." When done properly, this exercise should demonstrate how you have been moving sideways, not forward, even though you knew everything on the paper, because you've never approached it like this. You were accomplishing things separately, never all at once. You can't win unless you define what winning is and start working towards it. Once you do, it becomes possible.

NOTE: You can't have goals on your list that are actually impossible. You will not become a millionaire driving for Uber or Lyft. I have a saying: "To become a millionaire, you have to do something where you can make a million dollars." Driving rideshare ain't it. I had to cross "Spending more time with Zooey Deschanel" off my list, too, because nothing I was going to do driving was actually getting me closer to ever meeting Zooey Deschanel. So be realistic. (And Zooey, if you happen to be reading this, email me!)

What you've just created is a living document. Don't put it away. Keep it around. Read it often. Add and remove things as needed. You will find yourself actually accomplishing things that seemed like they were way off in the future.

And once you master being a rideshare driver, apply the same process to anything else you want to win at. It is much easier to win when you know what winning looks like.

"Be a 1st-rate version of yourself, instead of a 2nd-rate version of somebody else."
- Judy Garland

Signing Up

Basic Minimum Requirements

- 21 years old
- In-state driver's license
- Clean driving record with the DMV
- Pass a national and county background check
- A 4 door vehicle (with 5 working seatbelts) that passes inspection
- Cellphone: iOS - iPhone4 or newer, Android - 2103 model or newer.

There may be ways to get the cellphone and car through Uber and Lyft if you don't have them. Contact them or visit their website for more information.

Your car must also be within a specified age range, in terms of model, but that seems to vary by state. The model year minimum I've seen most recently is 2001-2006. If your car is less than 10 years old, you should be good. It has to have in-state current plates and tags and be currently insured as well.

Uber Signing Bonus

1. Go to **www.uber.com**
2. Press the "Become A Driver" button
3. Fill out the form with the Referral Code - VTY4V4GJUE

Referral codes are potentially a win-win, since in theory we both get a bonus; and once you have your own referral code, pass it around so you can get another bonus after a driver who enters your code takes their first ride.

Lyft Signing Bonus

Read this whole section before starting. Lyft is much more complex, even though the steps are simple:

1. Figure out what the options are and sort them by your preference.
2. If the referral is the best option, go to **https://www.lyft.com/drivers/CELEBDRIVER**
3. For other options:
   a. Follow the instructions listed with the option.
   b. Make sure the Promo Code field is not blank.

4. Fill out the rest of the form and submit it.

The referral bonus depends on the driver meeting some minimum number of rides in a certain number of days. That number may be crazy, like 500 in 60 days, and the reward the driver gets may be crazy as well: $2000. But Lyft is currently taking 25% of everything you earn, including bonuses, from them. This is deceptive, but you will rarely earn most of the bonuses offered, anyway. An experienced driver can do 500 rides in 60 days, but from the very start, they would have to average 60 rides a week. In my neighborhood, that would require 50 hours of driving a week, on average. Not impossible, but hard. For a new driver, a goal like this is pretty impossible.

However, there may be a smaller bonus offered that does not include a referral bonus. Why would I tell you to look for a way to sign up that includes no bonus for me? Because you bought this book, and in the end, I did not write this to benefit Uber or Lyft or even myself. I wrote it in an effort to help you get the best deal. Plus, most people are unlikely to complete the referral deal, at which point no one gets anything. Currently there is a deal where you can do 150 rides in 45 days and get $350. (I did that many rides in 35 days, driving part time with no incentive, so this is an attainable goal.) To find this deal, you may have to Google "Lyft New Driver Promotion."

There's one more important thing to note: Lyft limits their sign-up bonuses to the first 1000 or sometimes even less (in San Diego 500), and since they do not define the region, that may be nationwide. The only way to know if a promotion is still on is to try it. I tried multiple different promotion codes, and they were all rejected. I clicked on ads they were currently running and went to Google. Even though Lyft ads were plastered everywhere, none had a promotion code that would actually get you the deal they advertised. I thought in my last attempt that one had actually gone through, but Lyft claims the promo code field was empty. So I got no sign up bonus offer at all. It turns out that was foreshadowing for most of my bonus experiences with Lyft so far. Always be suspect of Lyft's bonuses and guarantees. I am guessing they have people working on how to offer you more and pay you less or nothing.

Try and make sure that you sign up with a promo in the promo code field. If none works, feel free to call them your favorite curse word. I did.

How long does it take?
From the moment you contact Uber or Lyft, it should take 5-7 days to get approved to drive. Note that that is not a hard and fast rule. If you are someone with a history of arrests, moving violations, and living in lots of different places, your application may take longer than someone with a clean

record who hasn't moved for 10 years. I would plan on 4 weeks. Hopefully, you will be pleasantly surprised.

NOTE: It took me 60 days, with little explanation as to why, to get approved by Uber. I have been clean and sober mostly since birth, and my only jail time was as part of a charity fundraiser. (I hope helping the Red Cross didn't count against me.) Lyft approved me within 24 hours of my orientation. This is an important example of why you should never choose sides. Drive for whichever company is best to you today. FREEDOM!

What does it cost to apply?

Currently there are no application fees.

What do I need to have to apply?

Of course you need access to a car that is insured; plus, all the paperwork with the state should be up to date. Your license and registration both have to have been issued in the state you will drive in.

I took my car in for inspection, and the mechanics made sure all the lights worked, including the blinkers and high beams. They also made sure all the seatbelts worked as well, two in the front and three in the back. Nothing fancy, but this could be something you can do yourself ahead of time, depending on how old your car is.

And have, or have a plan for, rideshare insurance. You don't need it to get approved but you need to have it before you start driving. See the chapter on insurance. This is complex. Make sure you understand it before you start.

Confidence

Remember that at every step of the process, you will have questions. Every single person has to go through it, and no one in your position has all the answers. You have to ask. This book is as close to a startup manual as you are going to get. Just know that when you don't know something, it is the company's fault, not yours. They are the ones who cut corners and don't have a formal manual for you.

Don't let the fear of not knowing what you are doing stop you. Be confident and don't be afraid to ask questions.

An Error I Made

When uploading pictures of my insurance and registration to Uber, I did not read the instructions closely. I did it twice, and I got emails saying they could not read my name both times. So I combed through the instructions for an answer - because the pictures were gorgeous - when I realized that in both pictures, the edge of the paper was just outside of each picture. The instructions specifically said to make sure all edges were visible in the picture. I took new pictures, submitted them, and got no error messages back. Important safety tip: follow the instructions.

"I have enough money to last me the rest of my life, unless I buy something."
- Jackie Mason

How Much Can I Make?

There is no one answer to that question. The answer is an equation with a lot of variables, some known, and some unknowable without actually driving. Here are a few:

- What is the density of your town? Not just population, but enough density to support you getting pings without having to drive 20 miles to pick up every passenger, or wait an hour or more for your second ride.

- What is a typical long trip in your town? In San Diego, you are unlikely to get a trip much longer than 40 miles unless you get an L.A. run (which rarely happens).

- How much are you paying for your car, gas and insurance?

- What kind of car do you drive? Does it qualify for a higher rate like UberBLACK or Lyft Premiere?

- When are you going to drive? Are the hours you drive the most profitable ones, or are they the ones most convenient for you?

Different Cities Have Different Rates

Let's compare UberX San Diego, where I live now, with UberX Ann Arbor, Michigan, where I lived for 25 years.

UberX	San Diego, CA	Ann Arbor, MI
Base Fare:	None	$1
Per Minute:	$0.15	$0.15
Per Mile:	$1.10	$0.90
Cancellation Fee:	$5	$5
Service Fees:	$1.95	$2

If you look at the table above, the rates are pretty similar. But the $0.20/mile difference looks pretty big. Let's run the numbers.

Full time drivers working in both cities will typically get paid for 1,000 hours in a year. You may go out for 40 hours/week x 50 weeks = 2,000 hours, but I estimate you will sit waiting for a ping on average about half of the time.

$$1,000 \text{ hours x } \$0.15/\text{minute x } 60 \text{ minutes x } 75\% = \$6,750$$

For argument's sake, I am going to estimate that a typical full time driver will drive about 50,000 miles a year. The reality is that you will likely get paid for only half of those miles. The other half are getting you to your starting point, getting you home, traveling to pick up a client, finding a restroom and getting gas. Your total take home is:

$$\text{Ann Arbor - } (25,000 \text{ miles x } 0.90/\text{mile}) + \$6,750 = \$29,250$$

$$\text{San Diego - } (25,000 \text{ miles x } 1.10/\text{mile}) + \$6,750 = \$34,250$$

That is what gets deposited in your account. Out of that, some things cost the same, or close enough, in both places (car loan/lease/rent, car maintenance, etc.) and some do not (gas and insurance). We are just focusing on the differences here (assume a 25 MPG car):

$$\text{Ann Arbor - } ((50,000 \text{ miles } / 25 \text{ MPG}) \text{ x } \$2.70/\text{gallon}) + \$600/\text{year}$$
$$\text{insurance} = \$6,000$$

$$\text{San Diego - } ((50,000 \text{ miles } / 25 \text{ MPG}) \text{ x } \$3.20/\text{gallon}) + \$1,800/\text{year}$$
$$\text{insurance} = \$8,200$$

Also, since your gross pay is higher in San Diego, you are likely to pay more taxes as well. Remember that most drivers will take the mileage deduction rather than itemizing, and that amount is the same across the country. Once you add it all up, the difference covers the costs but not much more.

Surge and Prime Time

That $5,000 difference in gross pay is important by itself, but it gets multiplied in importance by Uber's Surge and Lyft's Prime Time. Without the multipliers and bonuses, there would be a lot fewer drivers. They are needed to keep income at a level where drivers can justify it as an alternative to working the drive thru at McDonald's.

The reality is that without Surge and Prime Time, drivers would definitely be making less than minimum wage. Let's take San Diego for an example. The current minimum wage is $11.50/hour. That comes to around $23,000/year, plus benefits and the possibility of overtime.

Based on the government's assumption that a car costs $0.535/mile to maintain, that is $13,375. Subtract that from the $34,250 gross from above, and we are at $20,875. That is below the minimum wage, with no benefits and higher taxes (since you are a contractor). Surge and Prime Time offer the drivers the possibility of making more than minimum wage. It all depends on your luck in getting them.

The thing to remember is that putting in more hours does not increase your pay per hour. In fact, it should be the same or lower. You should already be driving the best hours you can, or at least be working on finding them. Once you are driving during high-demand hours, all added hours will pay you the same or less.

The way most drivers justify their pay is by ignoring the car's depreciation, thereby bleeding its value like a vampire sucking the life out of its victim. They put off an oil change, or run the tires past their mileage recommendation, cutting every corner they can. These drivers are livin' on a prayer.

Yet the reality is that there are estimates that say 50%-96% of the drivers quit every year, and only 50% of drivers drive more than 15 hours per week. It is tough out there, and we all need to avoid sugarcoating this fact.

But hang in there, because there are things you can do to maximize your return.

Your City Has Its Own Services and Rates

Each city has a set of rates for each vehicle class. If you don't know your city's rates, Uber and Lyft have them on their websites. Just Google "Uber/Lyft rates <your city name>."

How and When Do I Get Paid?

Once a week, your rideshare company will direct deposit your money into your bank account. Direct deposit rules!

Don't Base Decisions on What Other Drivers Tell You They Make

Most drivers don't know their own numbers. And when talking to them online, you often don't know what level of service they are driving for. Sometimes, they will tell you the gross revenue before the company takes out their cut. Some will quote their best week as if that was an average. Some drivers have a political agenda to get other drivers out of the business, so they say things to scare you. Some just make stuff up.

Talking strategy with other drivers is great, but talking numbers is likely a waste of time. Very few really know or want to know. Focus on knowing your own numbers and trying to improve them. Don't worry about what others are saying they make. More than likely, their numbers are off.

Bottom Line

It is impossible to have a bottom line for everyone. Where you live, what kind of car you drive, how many hours you put in, when those hours are, where you wait for your next passenger, and what days of the week you drive all play into that giant equation. Optimize all those factors, and you will optimize your pay.

Tips and Tricks for More Money

There are things you can do that will make the same effort result in more revenue. When I started, I made $8/hour take-home. Now I have a few months of experience, and I make $17/hour take-home while investing the same number of hours. I suspect that as I learn more about my city, I will do even better.

When

When you work also has a huge impact on how many passengers are calling for rides. Here are typically ideal hours to be working:

Monday - Wednesday	7am - 10am, 5pm - 7pm
Thursday	7am - 10am, 5pm - 1am
Friday	7am - 10am, 5pm - 3am
Saturday	5pm - 3am
Sunday	10am - 5pm

This will vary based on where you live and the people you are picking up.

Based on my informal conversations with other drivers (and reading a lot), it looks like Friday and Saturday are the busiest days to drive, so that is a good place to start.

NOTE: For me, the Saturday 11am-5pm time slot has high traffic as well. This is because there are a few colleges in the area, and the students need rides. Mix that in with people coming home from the mall nearby, and Saturday during the day is pretty active. This is what I am referring to when I say you need to figure out your plan based on your situation.

Another example of learning your city is that I discovered that 7pm-9pm on Friday and Saturday are usually slow. I almost always have a one hour block of sitting idle during those times, so I am driving different hours on different days to see how that goes. By experimenting with shifts, you will find the best hours to drive, and you should always drive during the best hours once you find them. The difference can be staggering.

Some drivers in bigger cities have had luck working off-hours, when most drivers are at home. Obviously, this is riskier, in that with fewer passengers, there is less of a chance that you will be nearby when they want to go. But test this out if the hours work for you. It might help you meet a goal.

Another thing to avoid is rush hour. Your per minute rate is not paying you minimum wage ignoring all your costs. Sitting in traffic with or without a passenger kills your hourly rate. Try and avoid it.

Where

I'm pretty sure that if my "go-to spot" was right outside my home, I would make a third of what I do by going where the people are. Are you downtown or in the suburbs? Downtown is great for short runs, when you need ride count for bonuses. The suburbs are great for having more down time and longer runs.

Uber itself has stated that 1 hour in the right place and time equals 3 hours in the wrong place and time. I imagine that has a lot to do with the difference between drivers who swear you can't make minimum wage driving and those doing better. You need to strive to be the right person, in the right place, at the right time. That sounds so familiar.

The time, day, and place information is different between Lyft and Uber. Don't assume they are the same. Different people use each service. For instance, I have found that University of California San Diego students seem to like Lyft better than Uber, so when I drive for Lyft, I head over to their campus to get my first ride.

An Exercise for the Reader - Finding Where and When

Go buy a spiral bound book with at least 168 pages of lined paper in it. Go through the pages and write at the top of the first page, "Monday 12 a.m." On the next page, write at the top, "Monday 1 a.m." and so forth. The reason it has to have 168 pages is: 24 hours x 7 days = 168 hours in a week. Every hour gets its own page, and every time you get a passenger, you record it on the page with the corresponding day and hour. Write the time and place you picked them up, and mark whether it was a repeating situation. (A repeating situation means that it happens in the same time and place every week.) For instance, you are sitting outside IBM at 5 p.m., and you get a ping. People are leaving work. The ultimate repeating situation. Another is the mall closing. Shoppers go home. Workers go home. Wash, rinse, repeat, write it down.

Now let's say you just hopped in the car after a well-deserved restroom break, and you see that 15 minutes from where you are, the train station is surging. Don't chase it. Write it down. Maybe you can integrate that surge in next week.

Don't Chase the Pink - There will be 8 drivers ahead of you in one spot when you get there. (Map data: Google, Lyft)

As your book starts to fill up, you can use it to make a plan. Before you start your day, look at where the busiest places seem to be for any given time. Make a plan for the day that keeps you in the busiest places with the most potential for surges. That plan is your base. You can of course add things, like when The Red Hot Chili Peppers are done playing at a concert hall, but remember this: your plan will change as soon as you get your first customer. Why? Because of where you dropped your passenger off. That was not in your plan. Do you drive back to where your plan had you next, or do you stay where you are and see if there is anything where you are? That depends. Are you in a place that does not look likely to have a passenger for you anytime soon? You have to make the call. But don't miss the opportunity of being someplace with which you are unfamiliar. Stay for 10 minutes to see if you get anything. Being paid to drive back is much better than driving back on your own dime.

An alternative exercise is to instead make the book place-based and highlight times when you see demand surging. Make each page a place and each line a time. Then this becomes your "go-to spot" book. When you need a place to go, look for what is close and should be surging soon.

When you are sitting, you should be watching the map on your phone and writing things down. You will get a better sense of when and where you should be driving every day. And when your book gets full enough, set it aside and start a new one. You need to keep up as things change. What works in winter may not work at all in summer. The only way you can figure that out is with a book.

I live in a college town, and I can tell you when the students leave town because my surges near campus drop to zero. That's when it's time to get a new book.

Places to Try Out

Are you near the airport when planes are landing? Are you near the stadium just before the game is over? Are you near the bars around closing time? Are you near the apartment complexes before school and work? The mall before it closes? Think of some other places and try them. Don't just drive around, but pick a spot based on what seems like it might work and go to it. You may find that even though a bunch of people need rides, a bunch of drivers are already there. You can use the passenger app to try to find a spot that is not covered.

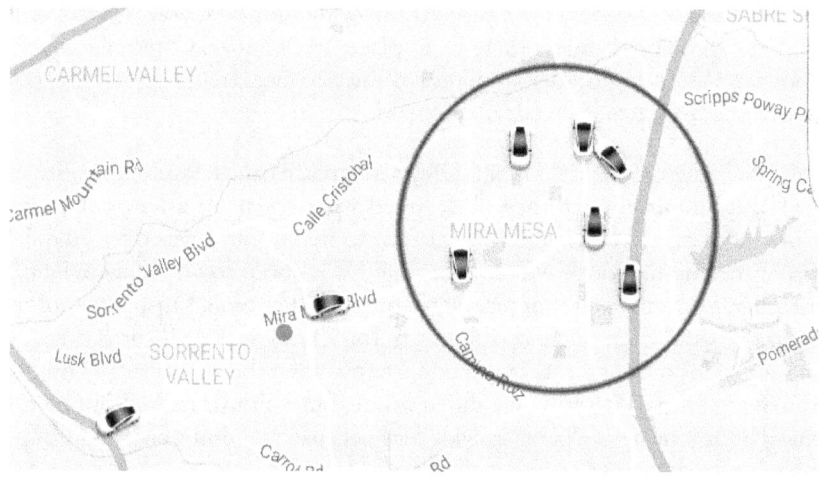

(Map data: Google, Lyft)

The above image is from a Wednesday night at around 8:45 p.m.. I am sitting at a Starbucks (using their wifi) and look at what I see. A bunch of nearby drivers are spread almost uniformly, as if they are working together. Obviously, they all believe that the rides coming up will all be on the upper right. Take this as a clue. Maybe it's just a good place in general. Maybe that WAS a good place, and drivers are hoping it will come alive again. Or maybe I am getting shown all the drivers who didn't get called, and the lower left is the better place. We should find out.

You need to take notes and test all areas. If you know of a good place to go right now, do that. If you don't know of one, have a list of places like this to try out.

NOTE: All drivers are playing the same game. Maybe they have knowledge you don't. Maybe they know nothing. But as someone trying to win the game, you need to see if there is something there. Not when there are six drivers there already, perhaps, but keep the location on a list of places to learn about.

Everything you do has to be dynamic. You can't make a plan that doesn't change for 10 years. If you don't have new locations to try and changes to your "best place to be right now" list every month, make sure you are looking at it carefully. You should be adding and dropping places every month. At the beginning, your list should change 80-90% every month. Later, it will only change 5-10%. Even if your list is good, you should always be testing and replacing your 5% worst times and places. You won't find the best gems without always looking for them.

One more thing: just because a place is throwing money at you for part of the day, don't stay all day unless there is no place that's better. Often places will be hot for 1-2 hours and dead the rest of the day. Feel free to nap there, but don't blame the place if you don't get paid.

I once got caught up north of San Diego in a place called San Marcos. I had heard of it but never been there. I dropped a passenger off after driving them for the most miles of any ride I had driven to that point. I was over 20 miles from home and had done well for the day. I was about to go offline when I got a ping. So I dropped that passenger off. Another ping. Dropped another person off - and both of those rides were for 10 miles each. It turns out that things are a lot more spread out in San Marcos than they are near my house. I was making money faster than I did at home, but I almost missed out by not waiting. Don't dismiss a place quickly just because you don't know it. I hope I get back to San Marcos soon.

You Don't Have To Make Every Dollar

This was the hardest lesson for me to soak in. Sometimes the best place to be is 20 minutes from where I am. I would drive there, do one run, it would dry up, and I would drive 20 minutes back. So I'd spent an hour to get one possible run. At best I broke even. Some days, I got nothing. Looking back, it would have actually been better for me to just sit for an hour and get no rides than it was for me to trick myself into thinking it was worth it.

How can sitting be better than moving? Simple - I always work on something while sitting. I work on this book. I work on my website. I work on training videos, sometimes writing scripts, sometimes shooting the video in the car. I work on finding a better place than where I am sitting right now for next week, or maybe even for tomorrow, by taking screenshots of where the other drivers are on the passenger app and where the surges are on the driver app.

You can also take breaks for food, restrooms, gas and cleaning up your car. Have a downtime checklist for when nobody is calling, or when you just need a break.

ABC - Always Be Cruising

That said, driving is for drivers. If you are not accepting passengers, turn off the app. The best way to make the most money is to accept a passenger every time you get pinged, if possible. Not accepting should only be done when necessary - as in, you are done driving and did not shut down the app quickly enough; and only cancel if you have a good reason like, you're running low on gas.

Cancelling to try and get surge pricing is a hit-or-miss prospect, and based on what I have seen, it balances out. If you take all the passengers you can, that will balance with the times you might have canceled and actually gotten a surge passenger. Don't try and game the surge. Having less cancellations is a better situation overall. Too many cancellations and they will give you a timeout. My motto is, "When they offer you money, take it." Your mileage may vary.

NOTE: *This does not include UberPOOL and Lyft Line. Those were designed for the companies to pay you less to do the same thing. Feel free to ignore those pings. Not only do you get paid less but the passengers are often much more demanding. Almost every non 5 star rating I have gotten is from someone trying to get a deal and not understanding that it may take up to twice as long or more to get where they are going.*

Pool vs X vs XL vs Select vs Black vs SUV

Uber has different categories based on the vehicle you drive. Lyft has a similar set of categories. Just replace the word Uber with the word Lyft in the following paragraphs and it is all the same.

Based on the category, you get paid a different rate, but the customer gets to ask for a car at a specific rate. So even if you are closer, if they are looking for an UberX car and you are only taking UberXL passengers, they won't even see you. You can go down levels if the upper levels are dry. Which category makes the most sense? That depends on your area. There's less demand for Black cars in Mississippi than in New York, but if you are the only Black car in Mississippi, well … you probably still won't get many calls. Gauge your area.

To provide a real world example, I just put in a ride, and these are the numbers. It is 12.8 miles, and Google Maps says it will take 23 minutes. The costs:

- Pool - $15.77
- X - $17.52
- XL - $31.00
- Select - $43.11
- Black - $61.93
- SUV - $79.74

The same ride, distance-wise, but nowhere near the same pay; the driver would get 75% of those amounts. To make more money you may want to look at vehicles that qualify for the higher pay services.

The thing to remember is that an XL vehicle will burn at least 50% more gas than an X type sedan, so having the option to drive XL comes with a cost. Without numbers about demand in your area, and how many drivers they have covering those rides, you are basically guessing. That is why most drivers start out with an X vehicle and move up when they have more knowledge about their area. Some even have two vehicles and switch. I don't know how or when they switch, but they do.

Downtime Checklist

_____ Get rid of garbage

_____ Wipe down your seats

_____ Straighten your floor mats

_____ Clean any windows that need it

_____ Spray some air freshener

_____ Roll down all your windows and let some fresh air in

_____ Make sure to write down potential "go-to spots" you spotted

_____ Mark down any spots currently surging

_____ Mark down if a surge ends

_____ Do something else that earns you money (videos, websites, etc.)

"There must be more to life than having everything." - Maurice Sendak

Bonuses and Surges

Getting bonuses and surges needs to be a priority. You have seen how just driving for normal wages is not enough, so mixed into your plan must be a strategy for how to take advantage of these options.

I often start my day by driving to the mall. Why? Because it's surrounded by apartment buildings with no parking. There are also hotels and offices nearby. It's a place that surges on and off all day, and it's about six miles from my home, so it's not a big commitment. About half the time, I get a ping before I even get there.

After a while, you should be able to predict how much you are going to make based on when, where, and for how long you are driving. There will be dry spots and busy times, but they will average out.

The game changing money from driving comes from watching for bonuses and surges. As I mentioned in a previous section, I am not an advocate of surge chasing. If you are a good distance away, the surge may be over by the time you get there, and then you just spent a lot of gas, in the best case, to pick someone up at the normal rate. In the worst case, you are staring at twelve other drivers and wondering where everyone is.

The key to making money is knowing where and when you can take advantage of a surge. When one happens, pull out your pen and paper and record it, and try and find a predictable pattern. That is the way to making more money. Be smarter. Know where the money will drop before it happens. Then be there when it falls.

One of the things I discovered was a concert venue that always surged when the concert ended, so I added it to my list of places and checked its schedule. If I was anywhere nearby when the concert finished, I went and parked close by.

Quiz

When should you stay out and when should you go home:

A. You have only driven for half the time you planned to, but you've already made your money goal.

B. You have driven all the time you planned to, but you haven't reached your money goal.

For A - You should stay out. You don't leave the table in Vegas until your luck has run out. The moment it does, you immediately get up and leave. Take the easy money, because tomorrow it may be hard.

For B - Unless you have to make the money, go home. Tomorrow may be better and you need to be ready when it is.

"I have an existential map. It has 'You Are Here' written all over it." - Steven Wright

Navigation

If you know every road in town, great for you. I previously lived in Ann Arbor, Michigan, a town of about 100,000 people, for 25 years and only knew about 50% of the roads from my own adventures. I delivered pizzas for a while, but there were just a lot of roads that I never knew existed. At least, that was true until I started driving airport shuttles. Then I was all over town, so eventually I was up to 75% knowledge of the roads. But never 100%.

I had to rely on getting directions for some places. Since it was an airport service, I knew my day's pickups and drop-offs before I started my shift. When I was in the office, I would go to a mapping website and print out the places I did not know.

Nowadays, of course, you can do that live with GPS software.

Software

There are two programs that most drivers use to navigate:

- Google Maps

- Waze

Try them out when you aren't on the clock and figure out which one works best for you. The only facts I can share are: Waze has more icons and ads getting in the way of seeing the map; and it lags more than Google Maps. Some people, though, swear Waze gets you there faster. Waze has a huge following of people who love it. As for me, I have learned not to question Waze except when it wants you to go the other way. It takes long routes when a U-turn would do. In the end, though, you have to choose for yourself. You can go online and watch one of the millions of videos that talk about both, but it's so easy to try them out on your own that there's no excuse not to.

Personal Knowledge

Before you start driving from your pick-up location, you can ask if your passenger has a special way to get to their place, or if you should just follow the GPS (unless you know the area well, in which case there's no need to ask).

Some drivers worry that they don't know the roads well enough to drive. Nonsense. Most passengers are fine with you using the GPS directions. For the few who aren't, when you ask, just tell them to guide you when you get close. Remember, you will be replaced one day by a GPS-following, self-driving car. Until that time, you rock.

Looking Ahead

Always have an idea of how far away your next turn is, and get in the proper lane early - anything to keep the tension level in the car down. Every once in awhile, I get into a situation where no one will let me change lanes. This can be even more tense for the passenger than the driver. I know I can get in by bullying my way over or slowing down until a reasonable person lets me in, but your passenger is just watching and hoping. Avoiding trouble is a 5 star move.

When the GPS Goes Nuts

Notice I didn't say "If." GPS software has its glitches. My GPS has one spot where it tells me to get off the highway, take a left, make a U-turn and get back on the same highway, going the same way I was going before I got off. Every single time. It never learns. Just know it might happen so that you don't freak when it does.

I have had it go crazy when I was downtown, too. The tall buildings, crowds, and many cars may each or in combination aggravate it.

If you start circling a block or doing something you know is wrong, you will have to switch software or, in Waze, you can just follow the directions and ignore the map. Know how to do that, and be prepared for that moment. If you drive enough, it will happen. My car has an in-car navigation system, so I am already running two sets of software. Most people don't have that luxury and have to stop to fix it. Know what to do by preparing for that moment when you don't have a passenger in the car. It isn't hard, but it can be if you are figuring out the steps with a passenger or three in back.

And ask your passenger for help. Often they will know the remainder of the way.

Effect on Rating

The thing that bugs passengers most is when you take a wrong turn and they think they are going to pay for it. Assure them that you will report what happened and that they will fix it. Making a wrong turn is the most consistent reason for a low rating. If you do it a lot, work on your system. Is the phone hard to see? Get a better phone mount. Is the software confusing? Try something else.

Pro Tip

Some drivers like to have a single Bluetooth earpiece in one ear to hear the audio from the GPS software - which is a courtesy, since passengers often don't want to hear the GPS talking during the whole trip. This way, you hear

it and the passenger does not. Plus, you can still hear the passenger.
Something to consider.

"Cleaning is simply finding a different place to put the dirt." - John C. Ardussi

Items You Should Have In Your Car

<rant on> I am now going to disagree with a lot of people and take a stand against the trend of turning rideshare cars into what I call "snack taxis." Having water available is fine, but I think that gum, candy or whatever you might be inclined to give to passengers works against you. I have a 5.0 rating with Uber and a 4.94 rating with Lyft, and I have no snacks available. In fact, I have water and have only had one passenger ask for it. That person was drunk, so I didn't give it to him. In general, don't give water to drunks, because it may not stay down. And don't offer passengers candy except maybe on Halloween. </rant off>

Essentials

This is where you spend your first dollars. Get these before moving on.

Phone

Required to run the driver software.

Phone Mount

Required to interact with your phone while driving.

Pen and Paper

Record your miles and potential hot spots, like bars to come back to later.

Vomit Bags

Drivers rarely need them. But when you do, you better have them.

Sun Glasses

Obvious. I got reading glasses-sunglasses and I can read the app much easier on my phone when I am driving. I carry regular reading glasses as well for nighttime.

Febreze/Ozium Air Sanitizer/Air Freshener Sticks/Diffuser

Something to clear the air. Pick one or more. People don't want to smell the previous passengers or the tuna sandwich you had for lunch. Make it so it is both something passengers like and something you can live with. I chose strawberry.

Small Towel

This is a towel that is there for messes. Paper towels also work.

Good Ideas

These items are good to have, but no hurry. As you get more seasoned, you can integrate them so that they are handy but out of the way.

Phone Chargers

These are also 5 star guarantee items, but the logistics totally depend on your vehicle. They are not expensive, so they're a plus for your passengers if you can offer them.

Audio Cable

Again, this depends on your car. A few years ago, I wanted a plug for my 2007 Mazda 6, and it would have been $75 to install it. My new car, meanwhile, has 2 plugs built into the center console. If you get to this feature, you are probably being rated as a 5 star driver by most passengers already, but if you can arrange it, it is definitely a good idea. You also may be able to use Bluetooth if you can't arrange a cable.

Flashlight

Finding house addresses at night can be a nightmare, even with the aid of a GPS, so having a flashlight can be helpful. Plus, if you or your passenger drops something at night outside your car, and you have a flashlight, you'll thank me later.

Facial Tissues

If you have the little Kleenex packets and someone arrives sneezing, you'll get 5 stars even if you run the car up onto the curb.

Paper Towels/Window Cleaner

Passengers like a clean car, and some like to take pictures out the windows, so have what you need to clean them. This will give you something to do in your down time that will help your rating.

Disinfecting Wipes

If someone spills something, and it gets on their hands, people will love you for having wipes. If the situation arises, 5 star rating guarantee.

Garbage Bags

Something simple to keep your car clean. They can just be old plastic bags from stores. No need to spend money.

Tumbler

Keeps drinks cold forever. Put ice in it and the ice will be there 8 hours later.

There must be some space shuttle tech involved or something. Whatever you drink will be cold longer than you can drive. I have a 30 oz. RTIC Stainless Steel Tumbler, and I alternate between soda and water during driving shifts. This saves me a fortune versus stopping to purchase a beverage.

Large Towel

You have to take service animals. No choice. Even if they have a cage, you'll want to cover the seats. This is an almost "Essential," but since it comes up so rarely, it is only a Good Idea. The reality is that you may never have an animal in your car.

Niceties

These items are not necessary but may be nice to have.

Napkins

In case somebody spills. Something for the seat pocket, if at all.

Umbrella

If it is raining, going and getting your passenger with an umbrella is a 5 star move. For me, the logistics don't seem to work out. Then again, I live in California, where it rains less often than in a lot of places. I have an umbrella, but I have not used it. Your mileage may vary.

Water

I carry this for me and stock enough for passengers, in case they want it. I used to put a bottle in the slot of each door until a passenger mentioned they thought it was left by the last passenger. It looked like trash to them. Now I keep a few bottles up front. People at the airport seem really dried out. Or, on a hot day, it can really be appreciated. But hand it to them. Don't leave them in the doors. If you have a back-of-the-seat place for it, that will work as well. This is a "depends on the day" item. For many drivers, they never do this. Your choice.

Snacks

Something to remember is that you are not a concession stand or a food truck. Handing out things costs you money. I have never done this. Some drivers do pass out hard candy, gum, whatever. This will not likely have any effect on how you get rated, unless it is Miley Cyrus you are picking up. In that case, you'll stop at Starbucks, and she'll take a grande nonfat white mocha, no whip.

Lint Brush

This is small enough and cheap enough that I have it in my car. If a cat or dog person gets out of your car, it can look like the pet got a ride, too. I have not used the lint brush, and I have had 2 dogs in my car, so it is just a "Nicety."

Hand Sanitizer

For the people who like to clean up after being in a public space - and if you are driving other people around, your back seat is a public space. Finding a place that is handy for this and not in the way is tough. If you've got a spot, go for it. If not, no one will miss it. One driver swears by it, so it made the list.

Microfiber Cloth

For that last minute polish/shine. This is nice for getting water spots off your car and the windshield after you use the washer fluid. The only down side is that your significant other might ask you to do their car as well. I have many. Love them. One of the things I use most, but not required.

Vacuum

You can have this in your car, or you may want to keep track of places around town that have good vacuums you can use. I used to leave it in my car but now I prefer the extra trunk space. Frankly, if I had a garage, I would keep it there. I would use a regular one at home, since the ones that plug into a wall outlet have a lot more suction. Your call.

Battery Backup

I use this so I can turn my car off and still power my devices. For me, this is Essential, but less so for almost everyone else. I also plug in my ear piece to recharge when I am not driving. There are solar powered ones, which seem like a good solution, since you can recharge it in your car, but mine is the kind you plug-in to recharge.

Video Recording Device

I have a recording device, but I don't know whether it is better to have one or not. It is an expensive item that for 99.99% of the drivers is unnecessary. The problem is, you don't know if you are in the 0.01% until something happens for which you need it. I don't tell passengers upfront that I have it. If they ask about it, I tell them that it is only for safety purposes, and they understand. I tell them that it records on a loop and erases old video with new video. I apologize and say that I won't be putting them up on YouTube unless they do something crazy. So far so good. It is a personal choice whether to get one or not. I would never try and convince anyone either way. In an emergency, you can use your phone if it isn't full of selfies.

Publicly, Uber has said they are okay with it. You should check to see if there are any state or local laws that apply.

"Americans will put up with anything provided it doesn't block traffic." - Dan Rather

The Best Car

The best car is:

a) The one you can afford

b) The one that generates the most profit

c) The one that does not break down

d) The one people are happy riding in

Answer: All of the above.

New vs. Used

I would never buy a new car for ridesharing unless I had some experience under my belt and knew the car that mathematically made sense for the job. That said, I had to buy a car because we only had one car. If I used our current car for driving, my wife would have limited ability to get where she wanted, especially on her days off. I did the math and showed her how getting a high MPG car would cover half the car payment (see Gas Mileage below) over driving our current car, and that I could get a car that was rideshare-friendly. She agreed.

Lately the difference in financing between new and used cars has been only slightly different. (When I was buying my first car years ago, used cars had payment amounts similar to new cars, but that was because I could get 3% on a new car and 9% on a used car. That was then.)

My credit union is currently financing used cars at 0.99% for 36 months, and 3.6% for 72 months. That is a crazy-great deal. The time you will spend paying down your loan should be the same as the span of time you expect to drive the car. Your loan should not outlive the car. If you can get a great used car, now is a great time to do it. You'll get more car for the same money, and you'll lose less when it depreciates than you would with a new car.

On the other hand, the tech of cars is advancing quickly. Our current car is a 2011, and there's no USB port in it. My new car has 2 USB ports and a three prong plug. It also has a built in navigation system and LED lights in the cup holders. I love my new car.

Buy vs. Lease

Leasing has its uses, but for most drivers it's almost assuredly a bad idea. Most leases have an extremely low mileage threshold, so you start paying for miles after 2-3 months. The mileage penalty will likely be at least twice what you pay for gas per mile. In some places, that means that you will be spending half of what Uber pays you per mile on miles and gas. Be careful. Any savings over buying the car will get eaten up fast.

That said, if someone can put together a lease deal and show me how it makes sense, I am open to listening.

Rent

Uber and Lyft have partners that will let you rent a car and buy insurance all in one shot. The good part about that is that it makes the math easier. You don't have to get each part and figure out how much you'll have to pay. The bad part is that what you will pay is probably 50% more than what you would pay to own the car, and you don't own the car. Even so, with discounts, and depending on your situation, this may be the best option for some people.

For renting to be a viable option, you have to drive full time or more. You have to earn the discounts, or the cars are too expensive to drive. I figured out that I would have to drive 12 hours a week just to pay for the cheapest car without the bonuses. Bonuses would cut the number of hours in half.

The best case scenario for renting is if you are a full time driver and your car is being fixed. The problem is that a car may not be available when you need it. They aren't Hertz. They don't have a lot full of cars waiting to be rented (at least not in San Diego).

Which brings us back to the math. Decide what you think is the most likely scenario for you. How long are you going to drive? A year? Two years? Longer? What are your car options? Put it all down on paper. If you are not sure you will last more than a couple months, then buying or leasing a car is a bad idea, and renting becomes the obvious answer.

Backseat Room

Just like on a plane, passengers need leg room. Make sure there is enough room for the person behind you.

Does the Color Matter?

Not much, as far as I can tell. I don't think that having a purple car will get you more or less money, but it will likely get you more smiles.

I bought a black car with a black interior - the same arrangement as my first car. That one was designed in the spirit of the battle cruiser from "The Hitchhiker's Guide to the Galaxy." It also reminds people of limos. That plays into the VIP experience I say that they're getting, but I don't think it got me an extra cent. They most often complimented the car's moon roof, but I am sure it has no monetary or star rating effect.

Gas Mileage

This matters a lot. For UberPOOL and UberX, you should try and get a vehicle that has 30+ MPG. For a long time, the Toyota Prius was the darling car of choice, not only for rideshare drivers but for taxis as well. Now, with SUV hybrids getting similar kinds of mileage, the options are expanding.

When you get into the higher paying classes, gas mileage is less important. You still should be getting 20+ MPG. Lower mileage than that in a car that Uber or Lyft would approve is getting harder to find.

Let's do some math: In Detroit you are paying about $2.10/gallon of gas (as of today, according to Gas Buddy). Let's say your car gets 21 MPG (to make the math easy). That means you are paying $0.10/mile for gasoline. Now let's say your alternative vehicle gets 35 MPG. Now you would only be paying $0.06/mile for gas. That means $0.04/mile more profit. Since the average rideshare driver drives 40hrs/week and about 4,000 miles in a month, that comes out to $160/month extra. I live in California, and gas is at $3.20/gallon right now. That means I have to be even more careful.

Estimating the Cost of Gas

$$\frac{(\text{\# of hours you work}) \times (\text{avg miles driven per hour}) \times (\text{price of gas})}{(\text{car MPG})}$$

You can use 25 for the average miles driven per hour for now. The other numbers are based on your situation and the car you are looking at driving. The thing to realize is that the 35 MPG car is basically $160/month cheaper than the 21 MPG car. Something to consider.

My Situation

I bought a loaded 2017 Ford C-Max SUV Crossover Hybrid. It gets 40 MPG combined city and highway. This is my cost of gas estimate (I average 24 hours of driving a week):

$$\frac{(96 \text{ hours/month} \times 25 \text{ miles/hour} \times \$3.20/\text{gallon})}{40 \text{ MPG}} = \$192/\text{month}$$

Now remember that that is the cost of gas for rideshare driving. If you use the car for other things, it will obviously cost more.

Pro Tip

I use Costco to fill up for gas. It is usually $0.40/gallon cheaper, saving me $24/month. This easily pays for the $55/year membership; plus, I can buy toilet paper in the convenient 48 roll pack while I'm there.

How to Make Even More Money

It is extremely unlikely that anyone will ever make $1,000,000 just by driving. My estimate indicates that even a fanatical crazy man driving 6 days a week/12 hours a day will need 10-15 years to make that in total - which means that driving rideshare is not a get-rich quick scheme. It isn't even a get-rich slow scheme. If we want to get beyond living paycheck to paycheck, we need some more options.

Another Job

I read that 80% of all drivers have another job, and 50% drive less than 15 hours. If you have another job, I would not quit it until you are sure this is going to pay enough to make it. In my case, I use it as a break. It is my replacement for not having a morning commute, but this way I get paid for my driving.

Always look for better opportunities. While driving you're exposed to lots of people, and hopefully you're in a stable financial position. Use that time and access to look for better things to do. That won't mean you have to stop driving, but maybe you can cut back to part time.

You can also promote your non-driving-related hobbies or skills via passengers. Maybe you build websites. Maybe you are a magician that does parties. Whatever you do, feel free to mention it to passengers and give them a card when they are getting out. But make sure not to overdo it. No one wants to be locked in a commercial they are paying for. Be sensitive.

Use Your Downtime

There are many things you can do while sitting in a car or at an outdoor table at Starbucks. Writing is what I do most. Watching rideshare driver training videos or reading my book would likely be a good one for you, but learning something new is a great way to go, too. I have heard of drivers getting their real estate license on the side; or you can become an IRS Enrolled Agent if you are into accounting.

WARNING: Reading or listening to political media while between rides (and even more so while driving) is a bad idea. The first thing you will want to do is talk with someone about it. You might get rated low just based on your political views and not the ride. Listen to music if you want something neutral to relax to.

If your passenger starts into politics, remember these go-to lines: "Good point" and "I understand."

Get Another Driving Job

In many places, there is a dry time between 10 a.m. and 4 p.m.. What comes during that time? Lunch! Uber just added UberEATS as a food delivery service. Check into that. Amazon has a Flex program where drivers deliver packages in their own vehicles. They use it as an alternative to FedEx, UPS and the Post Office. Check around. I am sure there are more. You can always sign up to drive pizza. They often pay more than Uber or Lyft and get much better tips. Seriously.

Referrals

The absolute easiest way for you to get more money is referrals. I'm not saying it will be a lot of money, but it's easy money. When you get approved to drive for Uber and Lyft, they assign you referral codes. Mine are below. When someone else uses them, you potentially get paid, so all you have to do is post them along with a reason why someone should use them. Then everyone else does the work.

Vistaprint and Lyft even have cards already set up. All you have to do is put in your referral code, pay for them, and pass them around. Leave some at a bar or a hotel. Here is a link:

http://www.vistaprint.com/studio.aspx?pf_id=B73&ep_template_id=97315

Uber and Lyft give something to the passenger and to you, so the passenger will be motivated to use it as well.

A potential big payoff involves signing up a new Uber driver using your referral code. This doesn't apply to Lyft, since that company's driver sign-up guarantees require the new driver to meet a certain number of rides (500 right now) in a certain timeframe (60 days right now). That would be possible for a veteran driver, but it's pretty hard for a new driver. Check to see if the current offer is easier. (It almost has to be.)

Uber requires the driver to actually drive 75 times and that is it. There's no time limit, and it worked the first time for me, so if you can, sign people up as Uber drivers for sure.

My codes for riders and drivers:

Lyft - CELEBDRIVER

Uber - VTY4V4GJUE

Just have people put them in the field listed as Promo Code, and you will get the current sign up bonus.

The current Uber driver bonus in San Diego is actually nothing. They are guaranteeing you will make $290 over 75 rides. Since I average around $8.50/ride, I would make $637.50 over 75 rides. Since that exceeds the guaranteed amount, I would get nothing.

The current Lyft bonus in San Diego is an actual bonus. You get an extra $2.26 per ride for the first 310 rides or the first 60 days, whichever comes first. But, from the terms - "This promotion is limited to the first 1,000 applicants. In San Diego, this promotion is limited to the first 500 applicants." So it is likely already no good. *<insert favorite swear word>*

Videos

Not a great money maker. You have to build up a huge following and produce 2-3 videos a week to get real money, but it's a great way to promote your referral codes and learn about driving.

I often say that the best way to learn something is to try and teach it to someone else. Pick a subject, maybe a chapter from this book, and do a bunch of research on it. Then try and explain your thoughts on the subject in a video. Say what you think, and don't be afraid to be wrong. Then post it on YouTube with your referral codes in the description and let the comments come in. Try and do one a month and see how it goes.

Advice for making your video:

- Stay on subject. Talk about one thing at a time.
- Don't use it as therapy. Talk about driving, not personal problems.
- Be positive. For 8 minutes act like your life is working out, even if you don't believe it.
- Cut out the pauses and flaws. Use editing software if you have to.
- Be conscious about what is in the frame.
- When you are done, stop. If the video is short, leave it short. Don't ramble to fill time.
- Thank people for watching and mention that your referral codes are in the description.

Write a Book

No, don't write a book. Okay, go ahead. I could use a little competition. Releasing a Kindle book is pretty easy nowadays. The rideshare fiction section is barren as well. I'm hoping someone will write "Lola Loves Lyft" and "50 Shades of Uber" soon.

Website

The website is the hub of everything. It doesn't have to be fancy. You just need one page with links for referrals, your videos, your book(s), and useful sites, like your favorite driver forums. There are a number of "build your own website" sites. I have my own site and use WordPress. Others use Wix, eHost and HostGator which include the site and the editing tools.

The Celeb Driver Website: **www.celebdriver.com**

If you want to get fancy, sign up as an Amazon affiliate and create a second page with links to items that you think are useful that drivers should have - things like your favorite window cleaner, or your favorite microfiber towels. When people use those links to buy the items, you get paid. Do the set up once, get paid many times.

Uber vs. Lyft vs ...

The question of which company is best to drive for is complex. Uber is bigger, better known, and has a lower deductible ($1000 vs. $2500 at this time) on their insurance if you get in an accident while driving for them. Lyft seems to have fewer drivers to compete with in my area, offers more bonus options, and has tipping built into their app. Uber does discourage tipping by not putting it in its app and advertising that you know what the ride will cost before you get in the car. Telling people they don't have to tip their driver discourages tipping, whether Uber admits it or not.

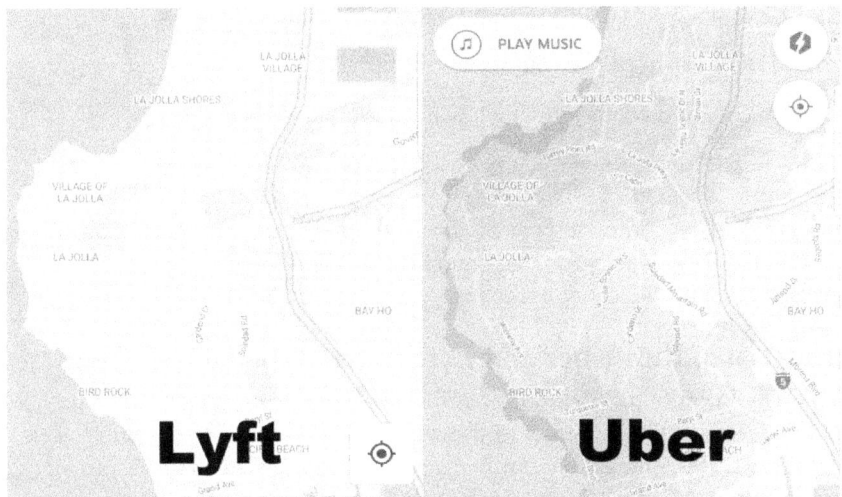

Grabbed at the same time. Which one would you choose if you were in La Jolla, CA?
(Map data: Google, Lyft, Uber)

Loyalty

If you've never worked for Southwest or Costco, then your employers likely had you around at their discretion. As soon as you weren't needed, you were out. Very few companies have a goal of not laying off workers. Steve Jobs once referred to Apple's layoffs as an opportunity for their workers to try working at other companies. Now that is expert spin.

DEBUNKED MYTH: Companies don't hire people because they have more money. Companies hire more people because they need more people. And when they don't need them, most companies will lay them off or fire them no matter how much money they have. Don't be more loyal to the company than the company is to you.

Companies like it when workers are loyal but rarely return the favor. I once worked nights and weekends for a job, and I saved a contract that saved the company from closing. I was laid off a month later. The people who created the hole I filled got to stay and ride the company into bankruptcy.

So don't let loyalty be a one-way street. Uber and Lyft are loyal to you in the same way that Disneyland is - If you don't cause a problem, you can stay. As long as you understand that, you're good.

Which One Should I Sign Up For?

Both. There is no penalty for driving for both. You are an independent contractor. Be independent.

- You will learn different things from the different apps

- You can see how you feel about tipping

- You get to find out which is busier in your town

- If one goes down, you have a backup

By signing up for both, you get the best situation for you. Even if you end up driving mostly or totally for one company, you still learn from your interactions with the other company.

How Can I Run Uber and Lyft Apps at the Same Time?

Generally I don't do this and here is why: in San Diego, the different services have surges at different places at different times. This has to do with the fact that Uber has 3-4 times the number of drivers in my area. (This is a total guess. No actual numbers are available, as far as I know.) But surges happen in more far-flung places with Uber than with Lyft. When Uber surges, you can see the Uber signs on the windshields as you drive towards them, so the best way to get surge pricing is to find the surge spots for each service and go there before a surge starts.

Now if I am at a Lyft surge spot with both apps running, I am highly likely to get an Uber ping. People there will be calling Uber too, just not enough to cause a surge. And some will price out both and choose the lower-priced option. I don't want to be the lower-priced option, so I find my spot and run only the app where I expect a surge.

When I started out, I used both apps more often. The reason was, I was documenting the surge areas of each app based on the time. To do this, it was easier to have two devices instead of one. I had a couple of old phones that would have worked, but I chose to use a Nexus7 tablet that I have because the screen is bigger. My favorite way to do this was to take a break from driving (when I had no idea where a surge might come), go to my favorite coffee place and use their wifi to document surge areas. When I would get out of my car to do this, I would stay offline on both apps. I did this for the first month. If I stayed in my car, I might go online for both since I had no idea which might hit first. But I almost never did that. Other drivers swear by it. You can see they have both symbols in their windshield when they pull up. I am more comfortable with one at a time. Just a personal choice.

"The insurance companies have reversed the business so that the public now insures them."
- Unknown

Insurance

Auto insurance companies have expanded their options to include coverage for rideshare drivers. Rideshare insurance adds coverage for at least some of the time that drivers are signed in to a ridesharing app.

Uber and Lyft insurance will cover your vehicle while you are driving a passenger. They may also cover your car if you are waiting to get called and are involved in an accident AND your regular insurance denies your claim. The reason I say "may" is that I am a driver, not an insurance expert, and after having dealt with insurance experts, I can tell you that insurance salespeople lie and mislead you to sell a policy. The only way to know for sure what your insurance covers is to file a claim. And I beg you to avoid being in an accident. Everything takes longer and is more inconvenient than you can imagine. The comfort of not being at fault will end as soon as you leave the accident site.

Will My Insurance Company Cover Me?

This is so complex and changing so fast that any specifics I write here will be wrong before you read it. So I have to speak about this in a general way, and you can see if it applies to you.

I was insured with a company that was infamous for dropping clients as soon as they found out they were driving for Uber and Lyft. An accident didn't even need to be involved for this to happen. I heard about someone who was calling to ask about doing the right thing and mentioned they were driving for Uber and got dropped immediately. I don't know that that happened, but I would guard against it anyway.

What companies support rideshare drivers? As of now, Allstate, MetLife, Progressive, State Farm, Farmers Insurance and GEICO all do in some states (look them up). I went with Metromile because they're pretty tight with Uber and seemed to be not hated in California.*

NOTE: When I went to Metromile to make sure that they were giving me the Uber discount, they told me that they no longer had a rideshare option and that my policy was for personal use only. They told me this even though I talked with them on the phone and said the only reason I was signing up with them was because of their deal with Uber. Did I mention that insurance agents lie to get you to sign up for their insurance? So I immediately dropped them and signed up with Farmers. There is now a line on my bill and amount of money I pay for Rideshare Insurance. That seems pretty solid but hopefully I will never find out.

The bad part is that very few people have good things to say about their insurance company. Why? Their biggest interaction with them is just after they were in an accident, and the insurance company is likely slowing things down. So getting reviews from others on insurance is hard. Every insurance company has (former) customers who think they are the devil. They may be right, but you still have to use one.

You can call your insurance company anonymously and ask theoretical questions about their policies. If they ask for your information, you don't have to give it to them. They do not need it to answer questions.

There are affordable solutions for most people at this point. Make sure to get this right. You don't want it all to unravel right when you need it.

What if there are no rideshare insurers in my state?

You will have to look into getting a commercial insurance policy. They cost more, but the limits are usually higher. You will have to do more research to see if there is anything that works for you. For some, it will cost too much, which may be a deal breaker. There's no point in driving so that everyone else gets paid and you get nothing.

Can I drive without telling my insurance company?

No. It may feel like you are getting away with something, but you won't find out until you make a claim. Insurance companies don't feel bad for you, and they won't cover you for things they are not obligated to. You might find out that even though you paid for insurance, you actually had no insurance because they do not insure rideshare drivers.

WARNING: NEVER LIE TO YOUR INSURANCE COMPANY. THAT IS FRAUD AND CAN LEAD TO FINES AND JAIL TIME.

Discounts

Make sure you get all the discounts. Here are a few to ask about:

- Equipment - Air Bags, Anti-Lock Brakes, Car Alarm, Daytime Running Lights.

- Safe driver/accident-free: A multi-year squeaky clean driving record.

- Driver's Ed for younger drivers.

- Full time students may qualify for a discount if they have a good academic record.

- Military service can qualify you for a discount.

- Low mileage: For keeping mileage down. Electronic monitoring of mileage may be required.

- Multi-vehicle, if you have another car, motorcycle, or motor home.

Look at all the insurance companies and ask around. Mostly try not to be in an accident. It is never a good thing to test to see how good your insurance is. They will usually disappoint.

Uber and Lyft Coverage

This table is a look at what Uber and Lyft cover as of this writing:

Company	Coverage limits with passengers / after accepting a ride request	Liability limits without passengers and before accepting a ride request	Comprehensive / Collision	Collision / Comprehensive Deductible
Uber	$1 million liability per incident; $1 million uninsured/underinsured motorist per incident	$50,000 per person, $100,000 per incident, $25,000 property damage	$50,000 (applies only with passengers)	$1,000
Lyft	$1 million liability per incident; $1 million uninsured/underinsured motorist per incident	$50,000 per person, $100,000 per incident, $25,000 property damage	$50,000 (applies only with passengers)	$2,500

What do I do if I'm in an accident?

If you are driving a passenger, or you are on your way to pick up a passenger, Uber and Lyft will be the insurer. When you go to trade insurance information, your information will be in the Waybill section of the app on your phone. You should have an idea where to find that before you go out.

You should expect that after you report the accident to the rideshare company, they will suspend your account while they investigate. I look at it as an addendum to your background check. If you have another approved car, drive for the other company for a while. Or, if you are a full time driver, look into renting a car with the other company as a short term option while your car is being fixed.

If your app is not on, or you weren't driving a passenger or to pick up a passenger, then your regular insurer is the one you contact and the one whose information you trade with the other driver involved in the accident. No need to contact Uber or Lyft. If you do, they will likely suspend your account while they investigate it.

If your incident is minor, such that the cost is not more than your deductible, consider just covering it yourself. It's your call, but there seems to be no point in contacting an insurer when they won't be involved. Treat it like a dinged door. I am not a lawyer, and this is not legal advice. It is just my opinion. I know there are people who will disagree.

Some people believe that their regular insurance will cover their deductible if they are not at fault, but I have not read that anywhere. That is a good question to ask when shopping around for insurance. Lyft's $2500 deductible is high. I personally keep my personal insurance with a $1000 deductible. Hopefully in the future, Uber and Lyft will create an option so drivers can pay that down. It wouldn't cost much, and I personally don't have an extra $2500 lying around in case I am in an accident.

Should I call the police?

If while still at the scene of the accident you estimate that the damage is enough that insurance will be involved, or that anyone has been hurt, then yes. The police might tell you that if no one is injured, you should just trade insurance info and move on, but call and ask. Sometimes they want to come and see if anything needs addressing, like glass or car parts in the street, if nothing else. If they come, ask if there will be a police report, and how you can get a copy. Then follow up and get one.

Filing

This is where being straight with your insurance company will help you sleep at night. If you are going to file a claim with your rideshare company, you have to tell your regular insurance company as well. In some states, all accidents are reported to the state, and your insurance company will periodically check. Again, I am not a lawyer, but it won't be a happy time when they find out.

Summary

If you can't do insurance without hiding something, you need to consider not driving. What might seem like a short term money solution may end up bankrupting you for years. Maybe even a decade. Spend the time upfront to do it right, or don't do it at all.

"The income tax has made more liars out of the American people than golf has."
- Will Rogers

Bookkeeping and Taxes

How and When do I get Paid?

You get paid once a week. The money you earn is direct deposited in your bank account.

Do I need a Separate Bank Account?

You can use your current bank account.

1099-MISC and 1099-K?

The 1099-MISC is the tax form that is sent to you and the government that says what the gross amount of money you received in the last year from them was. Everyone who gets money for work they have done without taxes being taken out gets one. If you go to the Uber driver software, it has an explanation of these that is better than I can do. I make video games, not accounting software.

Uber also has deals on tax preparation. It's definitely worthwhile to get help with the tax forms, or you can use TurboTax.

Quarterly Estimated Taxes

I am still not an accountant. But based on what I see, most people will owe between 0% and 15% of the money they take home in taxes. A lot of it depends on whether you file jointly as a married couple with another income. The closer the total (of your spouse's yearly income, plus half your driving income, plus any other income you have) is to $100,000 in the year, the closer you should be to the 15%. If it is more, then you need to pay more. The closer it is to $30,000, the closer you get to 0%. I would suggest you send in 1.25% x 4 quarters = 5% of your expected yearly income from driving as a minimum showing good faith, but again, I am still not an accountant.

Mileage vs. Expenses

Almost everyone will want to deduct mileage rather than itemize their expenses. One, it is simpler. You just have to keep track of your mileage. Two, it is likely a bigger deduction than if you itemize. But again, I am still not an accountant. Talk to a real accountant to get legit advice if you have any doubt.

Examples of Things You Can Write Off (so keep track of them)

These are the types of things you can write off, even if you take the mileage deduction. There are many more. If you used it for driving, you can write it off. Keep your receipts or credit card statements. Dedicate a credit card to these expenses if you can.

Car Loan Interest

An often overlooked item is the interest on your car loan. I believe this may apply to a lease as well.

Car Wash

Like a celebrity's clothes on the red carpet, maintaining how you look is a business expense you can deduct.

Car Detailing

A car wash on steroids and deductible for all the same reasons.

Supplies

All those things you have in your car: water, tissues, napkins, Febreze, etc. Save the receipts.

Phone

You cannot do your job without your phone, so you can write it off.

Phone Mount

You need it to do your job.

Cables

If you use them for passengers when you drive or to charge your phone, you can write them off.

Video Recording Device

If you have it on when you drive, you can deduct it.

Food

You can write off 50% of the cost of the food you buy to eat while driving.

The Price of this Book

Hey, it may get you a buck or two back. You are using it to improve your income.

If You Don't Take the Mileage Deduction - Itemizing

The mileage deduction covers a few things. If you don't take it, you can deduct these things separately.

Depreciation

The loss in value in your car based on age and mileage.

Car Loan Principle

This is the remainder of the loan payments that does not include the interest. If you pay more than your monthly payment to pay off your loan early, that is principle and can only be deducted if you itemize.

Maintenance

This includes gas, oil, tires, fluids, anything required to keep the car running.

Insurance

Your monthly premiums.

Full or Part Time (or More)

Driving is Not a Career

Uber and several car manufacturers (including Tesla and Ford) are talking about the day when people won't own cars. That might sound great for drivers, but their cars won't have a human driver. Computers will be driving their cars. Maybe as early as 2021 we will see the first autonomous rideshare program.

If you are young and need something to pay the bills, go ahead and sign up. Just know that it has a limited life span. Just like the mail room in large corporations, elevator operators, and gas station attendants, driving as an occupation will die off slowly. And as the jobs become fewer, the pay will go down.

But for now, eyes wide open, full steam ahead.

How Many Hours Is Optimal?

Obviously this depends on a lot. What are your money goals? What is your time availability? How flexible are you, time-wise? Would spending more time driving bring in significantly more money?

That last one is probably the one that will determine the answer of how many hours is optimal for most people. If you are doing your homework right and learning when and where to be for maximum money, then adding more time will likely be at a lower rate than your other hours. In some places, it may not, if it's busy enough. But in a lot of places, business is extremely slow for a significant part of the day, so balance your time and the payback to a level where you feel comfortable.

If you are spending days at a time not taking home at least minimum wage, you have to mix it up, cut back on your hours, and do something else during the slow times. Sign up for another service to fill in the gaps. Whatever it takes. Don't let the world define you. Show the world that you can kick its butt.

The key is to only drive when it is worth your time. If you drive to earn a certain amount per day, on slow days, you are likely to work a lot of hours. Then, when Saturday is on fire, you will be in bed, beaten and exhausted. Work the best hours first. Don't aim for an amount each day. You will end up with less overall if you do.

My Starting Checklist

_____ Have at least a half a tank of gas.

_____ Your vehicle is clean.

_____ Your vehicle smells okay.

_____ Your Uber and/or Lyft identifying cards are in the front and back windows.

_____ You have water and a snack for you.

_____ You brought what you wanted for your downtime.

_____ You have your phone in the phone mount and plugged in.

_____ Turn off wifi on your phone.

_____ Turn on Bluetooth on your phone.

_____ Make sure your mileage app is running, or you wrote your mileage down.

_____ Earpiece is charged.

_____ You are wearing your earpiece.

_____ Earpiece and phone are connected.

"It's the way you ride the trail that counts." - Dale Evans
My Ride Checklist

At the Start

_____ Unlock the doors as they walk up.

_____ Ask their name and make sure it matches.

_____ Would they like water/tissues/napkins? (If it seems like they might)

_____ Do they have a preferred route? (If it is not a place you are familiar with)

_____ If they are going to the airport, confirm which airline they will be flying with.

Once You Are Moving

_____ How is their day going?

_____ Music?

Before You Get There

_____ Tell them when you are a few minutes out, so they can get their stuff together.

_____ Explain the ratings system, if they don't know (5 = pass, 1-4 = degrees of fail).

Dropping Them Off

_____ Check for any items left behind. (often phones, keys, wallet)

_____ Thank them for being a great passenger, and tell them to have a great day.

Overall

_____ Do not talk too much.

_____ Do not talk too little.

_____ Be positive.

_____ Do not disagree on subjective topics like politics (say "I understand" or "Good point").

Dos and Don'ts

Don't Drive Around

Driving around helps fight boredom but costs you gas. A well-chosen spot to sit and wait is much better than driving around randomly. If you have a new destination because of an event getting out, that is different. Just don't drive around to occupy your mind. Do something else. Make a video. Make a website. Write a book. Okay, wait. Read a book. A much better idea.

If you want to drive around, force yourself to stay in each place at least 10 minutes to reduce your driving.

Don't Lose the Faith (in one day)

The worst thing you can do is quit because you had a bad day. Often a day will be slow just before it gets crazy. You get 2 hours of nothing and then a 30 mile trip hits you out of the blue. Ten years ago I was driving in Detroit, Michigan, and a huge snowstorm hit. I was ready to quit. I went out anyway, though, because I had nothing else to do. I got a $50 tip on a $20 fare because the passengers I drove were so grateful to arrive at their destination safely. Sometimes the worst times become the best times.

Now, if you are averaging less than minimum wage for a month, then it is time to question your faith. But even then, I have seen a bad month followed by my best month ever. I started in February, which was a lousy month. March was much better. You just have to be realistic with your expectations.

Don't Chase Surges, Document Them

If you find yourself in a surge or right next to one, take full advantage. But if you are a good distance away from a surge, try to figure out why it happened and what can you learn from it. Will it repeat? Will it happen similarly somewhere else? Did church just get out? Did the big movie having its opening weekend just end? Are the ponies done running for the day?

The way to win surges is to be there when they happen. Not to chase them. So your assignment is to anticipate them and win.

If you know why a surge is happening, and you do have time to take advantage of it with a little drive, go for it. There are no rules here. Just guidelines and suggestions. Try things and sometimes you will be rewarded. Usually, you will see why the guideline exists. These are both good things.

Do Find the Wealthy Areas

In Los Angeles, there are places I would not live if the rent was free. Then, just down the road, there's Beverly Hills; nearby is Bel Air; and up the coast is Malibu. Try and drive closer to where the wealthy people are because they will likely pay more and are more likely to call for a driver.

Do Listen

There is a phrase, "be present," which means that your mind is focused on the moment. For your passengers, you should try and be present for them. Listen to what they are saying, and comment to show you are listening and care. In a way, drivers are like bartenders/therapists. In this case, all you need to do is be a sympathetic ear and to comfort them for all they are going through. Don't try to solve their problems. Just listen and sympathize. But make sure and focus on driving as well. I have missed a few turns while fixing someone's life.

Do Maintain Your Car

Your vehicle is your money machine. Without it, you are not making money. Change your oil on time. Check your tire pressure monthly, especially in the spring and fall when temperatures are changing quickly. Have good windshield wipers and plenty of good quality washer fluid.

Be Ready to Quit

The worst thing you can do is try all my suggestions, keep making too little money, and keep fighting. No one from corporate headquarters is going to fly out to Podunk, Montana and give you a loyalty prize for being a financial martyr. If you can't make it work full time, dial back to your best hours and do something else for the remaining hours that pays you better. Lots of great drivers have done that. Maybe that is driving for Amazon Flex or delivering pizzas. Look around and see what is out there. Just don't be the rebel without a cause.

Boosting Your Rating

All You Should Do

You are a rideshare driver. You are not a food truck driver, a snack taxi driver, an ambulance driver, a pet taxi, a babysitter, or even a personal driver. You don't owe it to anyone to stop and wait while they go into a store. If they are thirsty, that is their problem. If they want a mint to cover their breath, why didn't they bring one?

Your job:

- Bring a clean/safe car inside and out that does not smell

- Be clean yourself and make sure you don't smell

- Be considerate, positive, and avoid confrontation

- Drive safely

- Get the passenger(s) there safely in a reasonable period of time

That is it. That is your total job. That is a 5 star performance, based on how the rideshare companies define the rating system.

Yet that is not how the rating system works in reality. There is a disconnect between the passengers and the companies. Why don't the companies fix this? The rating system functions well enough that the companies don't care that it is not accurate. The drivers are left to make sure to not get deactivated by a broken system.

The rating system is useless from the driver's point of view. Sixty 5 star ratings and forty 4 star ratings come out to a 4.6, thereby putting you on the bubble when the reality is that you are a great driver. Trolls are out there. I rang one woman's doorbell to let her know that I'd arrived, and she was on the phone the whole trip (5 miles in 12 minutes), and then she gave me a 3. This was early in my driving experience, so I only had two passengers that day, and it easy to do the math on my low rating. Why did she give me a 3? Did she seriously want me off the road? Was it because I went to the door and rang the bell? Or was she just annoyed that at the end of the trip, the GPS was not telling me where the store in the strip mall she wanted to be dropped off at was, forcing me to interrupt her phone call to ask? Or was it that the GPS took me the fastest way, not the shortest way? Or was it something else completely? I still don't know. For her, 3 stars might have been her way of saying it was just an average trip. Which should be okay but isn't.

Keep Your Car Clean

If your car is dirty (inside and out) or smells, a 5 star rating is a gift. Do your best. Sometimes fate intervenes and we fail on this one. Just make sure you're good before your first run every day.

If there is a do-it-yourself spray car wash, spend a couple bucks before the start of your driving day and wash the outside of the car if it's dirty.

Get the Snow and Ice off Your Windows

Use a mixture of one third rubbing alcohol and two thirds water in a spray bottle and spray the windows before you go out for your first run. You can keep the bottle in your car because the rubbing alcohol will keep it from freezing. Ice on the windows can look sloppy, even if it does not interfere with your driving.

Clothes

Always dress as if you are picking up a representative of the company you are driving for, because on any given day, you might just be. I recommend relaxed office dress or better. For guys, a tie is not required, but it's not a bad idea if you are driving UberSELECT, UberBLACK, Lyft Premiere or Lux. For women, don't wear a skirt or heels. You will be getting in and out of the car all day. And everyone needs to wear comfortable shoes for driving.

Make sure your clothes are ironed - nothing off the top of the dirty clothes pile. Show your passenger respect, and they will recognize it.

UPDATE: I started wearing nice shorts and my ratings went up. Pretty much a 5.0 since then. Everything is clean and pressed but more relaxed. Go figure.

Picking Your Clients

These are desperation maneuvers. After your first 100 rides, if your rating gets below 4.7, you need some drastic measures.

1) Never pick up a 4.7 or lower rated passenger. How hard is it to be a 4.9 passenger?

2) Before you get to their destination, ask if there is anything you can do better.

Like I said, these are desperation maneuvers and should not be used if your rating is fine. It will hit your bottom line when you are passing up passengers that would likely rate you just fine. Asking about what you can do better implies you can do things better, so pick and choose who you ask carefully, and listen to them. If you're talking, you're not learning.

Arriving for Pick Up

If you are at a public place, like an airport or bar, ask their name before you start the ride. Getting this routine down is important, because you will have someone hop into your car at some point who is not the person you are there to pick up.

Once you have the right passenger, ask if they know a better way to their destination - if it is a place with which you are unfamiliar. This is often a good thing. They will almost always say "No." When they don't say "No," it is likely they are correct, so listen to them. Wrong turns are a top reason for getting a low rating. And if you don't go their way and get stuck in traffic, it's on you.

Bags

If you can offer to put a passenger's bags in the back of your car, do it. I am a big guy, and I guarantee you that if I don't put the bags in the car for a smaller woman, I am not getting a 5 star rating. I know it isn't company policy (I could not find one on this point), and I know I am going a little rogue by telling you this. Is it right that people will rate you lower for something you should not be required to do? No. Will they do it anyway? Yes. Can you appeal? No. You are never told what rating you get from any individual passenger or why. You can't appeal things when you have no facts.

That said, don't risk your health. If you might hurt yourself, you have to let them load their baggage. You have no disability coverage, and if you get hurt, you could end up out of work for a while. Feel free to cancel on them if their bags are just too heavy, and no one can get them in the car without risking injury.

I had one male passenger who could not lift his own bag. He was moving his books. I am guessing the bag weighed 75 pounds. He was lucky he got me as a driver. If refusing to help him would have sent a message to the world not to do this, I would have canceled on him. However, since it was just me and him, I loaded it for him.

Small Talk

After you get all the trip details so you can drive (like what airline they're flying with at the airport) and the car is moving, just ask how they are doing. Based on how that goes, either keep talking or let them have a quiet trip. Some people like to talk about themselves. Others like quiet. If they look like they are on the phone or texting, no need to say anything.

If you feel it is too quiet, offer music. But make sure you do what they want.

Be Little Miss Sunshine

The reality is that you are in these people's lives for approximately 5-50 minutes and will never see them again. How is your day going? Get a Thesaurus and look up the word "great." Be positive. Mention that you might pick up a lottery ticket, things are going so well today. If the weather is nice out, mention how that is a plus. If the weather is bad, mention how your day is great in spite of the weather. Mention how everyone is being nice to you today. For them, your life is good. They are not there to fix your life, but they are more than happy to be a part of a success story. Let them feel they are, whether this is how you feel or not.

Explaining the Rating System to Clients

When regular people see the rating system for the first time, they think ratings are like grades: 1-5 stars equal A-E grades. Consequently, they think a B (or 4 star) rating is good, and they think they are doing you a favor by giving you 4 stars. You have to explain to them that 5 stars equals "pass" and 1-4 stars is a "fail." Tell them that the way the company uses their rating is not how they would likely expect, which is why you like to explain it to people. Make the conversation quick, and once they understand it, move on to something else.

I don't lobby in conversation for a 5 star rating. I do lobby in my business cards and marketing materials (website, etc.) by saying I try to create a 5 star experience. Mention that you keep your car clean and anything else you do to make their experience better.

If you want to lobby for 5 stars, just tell the passenger that you like getting feedback on anything you might do to make the ride better. If they do or don't suggest anything, that should mean a 5 star rating (unless they are a troll).

Arriving at Destination

Make sure to give your passenger a heads-up before you arrive at their destination. They may want to call or text someone. But don't disturb them if they are on the phone.

Be Gracious

Thank your passenger for calling for you.

Always Acknowledge Their Thought

Never argue. If they say something you disagree with, you can always respond, "Good point." I once had to sit through an entire haircut with talk radio blaring and a barber who wanted an armed revolution. Never provoke a man standing behind you with sharp tools. And there is no gain from provoking a passenger who is about to rate you.

"The needs of the many outweigh the needs of the few, or the one."

As a driver driving your own car, it can be hard to see yourself as a representative of a large corporation. You may not know the names of any people actually working for the corporation. So you have to be better than your gut probably will tell you to be. As I mentioned above, you have to let stuff go. Why? Because no corporation will ever be the fair distributer of justice. That is not their goal or focus. It is the goal of the police, and they have a hard time with it as a full time job. So some people will get the bad end of the stick when they did nothing wrong. It just happens.

Knowing that, the best thing you can do is avoid bad situations as much as you can. If someone starts to get upset, agree with them and drop them off. Here is a scene from *"Two and a Half Men"* that explains it well:

Alan: Charlie, when I moved in here, I said that is was vital that we create a wholesome atmosphere for Jake, and you said, "I understand".

Charlie: Alan, there's something you should know about me. When I say "I understand", it doesn't mean I agree. It doesn't mean I understand. It doesn't even mean I'm listening to you.

Alan: Then why do you say it.

Charlie: It seems to make people happy. That's what I'm all about.

"If They Do Go Either Way, They're Usually Fake", Two and a Half Men, Season 1, Episode 7

While voicing what seems like a perfectly reasonable response, or engaging with a crazy man, may feel right, you create an incident. Incidents are resolved by someone who was not there. Someone whose interests are in the 1,000,000 other drivers over yours. The many versus the few, or the one. When Uber, Lyft or any large corporation is involved, you should always try to be in the many and never be the one. The one almost always loses.

In sports, they have a saying that you don't leave the fate of the game in the hands of the refs. The refs will get it wrong sometimes, even with instant replay. It is so much better to avoid the whole thing.

And Finally

Do not take your rating as a reflection on you. Do your best, and let the ratings fall where they may. Once you have 100 ratings, no single passenger can sabotage you. And corporate pays little attention to your rating until you reach 100 rides. You should do the same.

"Success is not final, failure is not fatal: it is the courage to continue that counts." -
Winston Churchill

The Biggest Mistakes I Know Of

Picking Up the Wrong Passenger

This is one of the easiest and most common mistakes drivers and passengers make. It most often happens in places where 2 or more people are calling for a car at the same time. The reason is simple: everyone hopes their car will show up first and that they can get going quickly. So when it does, they often don't check to make sure it's the right car. If you do two things, you should be able to avoid this:

1) Ask their name, do not confirm it. "What is your name?" vs. "Is your name Chuck?" Sometimes passengers think they can get away with "stealing" someone else's car, but it won't work.

2) Confirm where they are going. The right name works almost all the time. The right destination gets the remainder. You can say "Are you going to Country Mountain Road?" because the odds of two guys named Chuck coming out of the same place and going to the same street are astronomical. We are talking a *"Star Trek* transporter accident creating two clones" impossible. So you should be good.

If someone gets into your car and you are sure they are the wrong person, ask them to get out so you can pick up your passenger. If they have ordered a car, suggest they check for their car before someone else grabs it. Make it clear that you cannot take them. They cannot affect your rating, since you are not their driver.

Not Knowing the Software

The time to be figuring things out is not when you have a passenger in your car. Get yourself familiar with things when you are off the clock, especially your GPS software. Get familiar with how to use it. Get the voice volume right, get your ear piece working, or turn it off completely. Play with the software when you are alone and running errands, like going to the grocery store. You know the way, so you can see what it says and set your expectations appropriately.

Not Being Ready to Drive

At the start of the day, have as many things as ready as possible. What's the longest drive you can expect to pick up from where you are? That should not include the crazy "I'm going to Vegas, baby!" requests that are like lotto tickets. What I am talking about are the typically long runs. How far are you from the airport? Do you have enough gas to get there and then some? Do you have water? Not just for the passengers, but for yourself as well? Can you wait to eat until you drop them off? Did you pee before leaving?

If you are not ready, sign out of the driver app, get ready, and then sign back in. This is not an endurance match to see who can stretch their bladder the most. You are an adult now. Be ready.

Not Having a Plan for Gas, Food, and Bathroom Breaks

Where do you buy gas when you get low? Are you driving over a mealtime? What are you going to eat? If you are 30 miles from your house, where will you go to the bathroom if you have to go?

Most cars get 400+ miles on a tank of gas. Most drivers drive less than 200 miles in a day. If your tank is below half, make a plan for when you will fill up.

Always have a snack handy. Maybe gum, hard candy or chocolates. That way, if you keep getting passengers and can't eat the sandwich you brought, you can snack on something non-offensive to your passengers.

Gas stations can be hit-or-miss on whether they have a working bathroom. Fast food places are usually guaranteed, although some have locks. Some drivers use adult diapers, and others carry a pee jar. While I recommend neither, they are better than trying to get the pee smell out of your car.

Think about these things ahead of time so you don't have to make a decision on the fly.

"Do or do not, there is no try." - Yoda, "The Empire Strikes Back"

Reasons Uber and Lyft Would Drop You

While none of these are likely to happen to you, it is always good to know where the lines are.

Violating the Code of Conduct

Uber has a list of things they want you to follow. (Lyft, I am sure, has a similar list.) If you don't follow these rules, you risk getting the boot. Here are a few highlights:

- Keep your language clean

- Drive safely

- Don't break the law

- Don't have inappropriate interactions with customers (aka would your mom approve?)

- No drugs or alcohol while driving

- No carrying firearms

- No fraud, as in gaming the system to make more money

- No fraud, as in lying about license, registration, insurance or what car you are driving

- No discrimination based on where they are going or personal characteristics

A Co-pilot

Some people feel safer having a friend ride along and some just want someone to talk with during the down times. Bad idea. If the passenger leaves feedback mentioning this, you are done. No exceptions. And yes, this includes pets.

Driver Rating

Right now it looks like a 4.8 rating is average, and 4.6 or lower gets you third prize - you get suspended and reviewed. There are third party classes you can take to get reinstated, but I know nothing of it. Hopefully you never will either. Read the section on boosting your ratings and do that.

Documentation Not Up To Date

Make sure to always keep these up-to-date, both generally and on the Uber and Lyft websites:

- License

- Registration

- Insurance

Not keeping them up-to-date will likely cause Uber or Lyft to deactivate you. Once you get the information updated, it may take a week or two for them to reactivate you. Definitely something to avoid. Post the information as soon as you have it.

Not Driving

If you don't drive for 90 days, they take you off the books. You can take that 2 week vacation and not worry, but much more than that and I would make a few runs. They will also contact you via email if you are cutting it close, so make sure and read the emails they send you.

Driving a Different Vehicle

Imagine as a passenger you called for a BMW, and a 1976 AMC Pacer shows up. Not cool. All vehicles you drive must be inspected and added to your account. And make sure the system knows which one you are driving at any given time.

Getting Convicted of a Crime or a DUI

A lot of bad things happen when you get convicted of a crime. If this is a problem for you, heed Jim Carrey's advice from the 1997 movie *"Liar, Liar"*: "STOP BREAKING THE LAW!"

In all seriousness, try and avoid trouble. That does not mean running away from the police at high speeds. Do your best to stay clean. This is an opportunity. Don't blow it.

Cheating For Bonuses

I have heard that drivers have used their own account to drive themselves to get bonuses, and it didn't go well. Others have used two phones to maximize surge opportunities. But if it seems like cheating, then it likely is cheating and can get you dropped if you get caught. The companies have ways of comparing GPS locations (among other things) to detect cheating. Don't do it.

Safety

If you drive in a way that scares your passenger, they may report you.

Obviously, driving drunk is no good, even if you don't get a ticket. I heard about a guy who was saying inappropriate things to his single female passengers. They reported him and he got deactivated. Treat all your passengers with respect.

Unfairly Criticizing Uber or Lyft

Social media postings are available to the planet. Don't assume that if you say bad things about Uber and Lyft that they won't find out. I have not heard of anyone terminated for this, but I can imagine it happening. My guess is that if you are honest and don't troll them, you're good, even if what you say is not flattering. (Here's to hoping! Fingers crossed!)

Promoting a Different Service

If you're driving for Uber when your car has "Lyft" painted on the side, or when you hand out Lyft business cards, or when you're wearing a t-shirt that says "I would rather Lyft", who could blame Uber for being displeased? If you want to promote another service, hide all that stuff when you drive for Uber. Did you hear that Kate Upton was banned from wearing a Tigers hat in Yankee Stadium? Do the classy thing for the people who are helping you make money. Simple enough.

Not Obeying the Law

The worst thing to have happen is to not be able to drive, or to get a huge ticket because you went along with a passenger's request. Even if they pay the fine, it's on your record. No amount of money will fix that, so no single trip is worth the risk. None.

To get an idea of things that can happen, talk to other drivers, or go on driver forums and ask questions. Join driver Facebook groups. If you think about these things ahead of time, you'll be more confident in your reaction and more likely to do the right thing.

Here are a few examples of what I am talking about:

Alcohol

It must be closed and I have them put it in the trunk. Passengers cannot have opened alcohol as well. No arguments. It is the law. Uber and Lyft have a zero tolerance policy on drugs and alcohol. Don't test it.

Animals

It is a Federal law that you cannot refuse to take a service animal, which is why I recommend having a towel to cover your seats. Know the law in your state and follow it. Not following it can jeopardize your status.

NOTE: If you cancel because of a service animal and an allergy, you may still be deactivated permanently. It is a Federal law and has no allowances or exceptions.

Pets are a different story. Uber has made a statement for passengers about pets: "Use your app to send a text message or call to let the driver know you'd like to bring a pet. Please help drivers keep vehicles clean for all riders by bringing a crate or blanket to reduce the risk of damage or mess. Some drivers may keep a blanket in the trunk."

Once you arrive to pick them up, evaluate the situation then. If it is an unfriendly dog that is not in a cage, I would cancel. Remember that no single trip is worth risking your vehicle or your health.

Assistive Devices

If you can accommodate items such as a walker, cane, folding wheelchair and the like, you must do so. If the device will not fit in your car without sticking out or interfering with driving, or is too heavy to get into your vehicle, cancel the ride and recommend that they ask for a larger class of vehicle. Uber has a service called UberASSIST that costs the same as UberX but includes vehicles and drivers that have been cleared to handle special needs cases.

I actually had a wheelchair that I was sure would not fit in my vehicle, and there were four passengers, so no seats could go down. Then one of the women fit it in easily. She'd folded all the parts in that would collapse, and it wasn't even tough. I'd remained skeptical but hopeful the whole time and was pleasantly surprised. Remember that the people that use these devices daily have experience and often know better than you.

"If you reveal your secrets to the wind, you should not blame the wind for revealing them to the trees." - Khalil Gibran

The Dirty Secret No One is Talking About

I have watched hundreds of online videos, and I've read many Kindle books and blogs, and I have never heard anyone discuss this subject: saturation. Some of the material references the effect, but never by name. They say something like, "You don't want to drive when there aren't many passengers," or "Look for the surges." They never present or explain this formula:

$$\text{Saturation} = \text{number of passengers} / \text{number of drivers}$$

The ideal situation for the company is when saturation equals 1.0. For drivers, saturation greater than 1 means surge. Saturation of less than 1 means drivers sit and wait. The best situation in general is when the number of passengers and drivers are in balance.

You might say, "But surge is good for drivers." Not long-term. If riding is expensive, and passengers have to wait longer for a driver to arrive, over time, passengers will find an alternative. This will lead to fewer passengers at other times. To see how the "fewer drivers than passengers and higher prices" thing works out, see "taxis."

Yes, if a surge is there, take advantage of it. But understand that Uber and Lyft are trying to reduce the number of surges to increase the number of passengers. And just like the regular customer at the coffee shop, your favorite passenger is the regular passenger. To get them, they need consistency and affordability. You should support that. If you are driving again after today, it is in your long-term interest.

Don't boycott Uber or Lyft because their overpaid marketing people are stumbling around trying to find a policy that doesn't offend people as they explain it poorly. UberPOOL is a great example of this. They said that drivers would make more money and they don't. As a driver you can tell this is false after one drive. But the answer is not to stop driving.

Tell them what you think, even refuse to take UberPOOL passengers, but remember: you are on the same team. As long as it is just awkward and inconvenient, don't stop working with them completely. They'll get their act together. This is all new. Remember: the defense doesn't quit when the offense turns over the ball. They work harder to get the ball back.

Now here is the bad part no one is talking about: what if your saturation number where you are sitting is less than 1 all the time? This can happen for 2 reasons:

- There are too many drivers.
- There aren't enough passengers.

Notice there are no numbers in those two statements. Too many drivers in some places, like Empty Field, Idaho, might be one. And too few passengers in Los Angeles could be 4,000, if you have 10,000 drivers waiting for them.

One of my goals in writing this book is to get you to identify places where the saturation number is higher. That is the key as a driver to making more money. Compare it to the stock market. You don't want to just buy a stock. You want to buy a stock that's going up. My job is to give you the tools to find the best stocks. In this case, a stock is the time of day at a particular spot, based on the day of the week.

My message to Uber and Lyft

Just like the coffee shop, rideshare companies should be encouraging the regular customer with discounts and specials for use. After they spend $100 they get a $5 discount automatically on their next ride. And send them Thank You cards at Christmas if they spend over $1,000 in the year. Unexpected bonuses are the best kind.

Also, focus on tools to reduce the driver over-saturation numbers when appropriate. Create tools that tell drivers when they are in a rideshare dead zone, so they can have the option of moving, sleeping, or visiting their family rather than sitting in their car, hoping their phone will beep when there's little chance it will. Have an oversaturation indicator, which is the opposite of surge. You have the data. You know surge. You know drought as well. Pass it along. Show the drivers you are on their side. And send them a birthday card, for goodness' sake.

"Any sufficiently advanced technology is indistinguishable from magic." - Arthur C. Clarke

Advanced Topics

These are small topics that nonetheless need to be covered.

Returning Items Left In Your Car

If someone leaves something in your car, offer to let them come pick it up. You have no obligation to take it to them. Meet them at a Starbucks or some other public place (the police station has been suggested). Give them a 10 minute window.

You can also take it the company's local office. I have heard of mailing it, but I did not find any official discussion of that. I would contact the company's help desk and ask if it comes up.

Do not return drugs, weapons, bags of money or anything that looks like it may be something involved in a crime. And don't touch them if possible. Take those to the police.

Passengers are responsible for not leaving things in your car. You're not responsible to return items to them. Make a small effort. If they can't meet that, offer to tape it to the back of a Stop sign and tell them where they can find it.

WARNING: Okay, ignore that last bit. I get tired of people messing up and expecting me to fix it. They can fix it. You owe them nothing. Give them an opportunity to fix it but with minimal time and expense on your part. I am not sure why the police feel that paying you for your time and effort is ransom, but they do, so do not ask for money. For some reason, driving people for money is okay, but driving the stuff they lost for money is extortion. If Uber and Lyft want a better system for handling lost items, they should create it, and they should pay for it. They should not leave it to the drivers to handle it.

My solution; put it in a sealed envelope and have the person get another rideshare car to deliver it to them. I know this sounds the same as paying me to deliver it, but as far as the police go, they are fine having someone else get paid, not me. People send items and food by themselves via Uber and Lyft all the time. Why not their wallet or phone? And if my being paid to deliver it is extortion, pay someone else. Or do the stop sign thing (kidding - mostly).

Bathroom Breaks

If you have to go to the bathroom, you are on your own. Drivers are left to figure out how to pace themselves so they don't have to pee while driving passengers. There is no pause button on the driver app, nor will the GPS help you find a bathroom. I guarantee you that if either of the driver apps were open-source, that would be one of the first features added.

The Airport

All airports are different, so there is little advice that works at them all. For instance, sometimes you have no access at all, and you have to drop people across the street and have them walk. You have to find your airport's rules and read them. The number one rule that applies to all airports is that they are patrolled and give out fines. If you don't want to get a fine, learn to follow the rules. I had to post Google Maps satellite pictures of the San Diego airport in a local Facebook group, after drawing my paths, and ask if I got it right. It took a while, but a few people finally confirmed that I had it right.

Military Bases

San Diego has a few, so I know the rules. You cannot pick someone up on base, so they have to meet you at the gate. Sometimes they will let you drop people off inside the base, but not always. Do whatever they tell you at the gate. Even if you think they are wrong, or what they are doing is different than before, do not argue. They are the law on the base and can ruin your day on a whim. You don't play chicken with a brick wall, and you never cross the Military Police.

WARNING: If the pin is inside the base, you will not get credit for arriving. If the passenger is not there and you cancel, you will not get a fee because you did not go to the pin. You can't. And some people abuse this. I waited 10 minutes and they never showed. I canceled but did not get a cancel fee. I sent a complaint to Uber and got robo messages saying my case did not qualify me for a fee, but did not say why. So I avoid the bases now. Military personnel are some of the best passengers, but I am doing this to make money. If they want to have me pick them up, just meet me off base. You pretty much have to anyway.

Multiple Destinations for One Customer

Passengers will often ask to stop at a store before going home. This is totally fine from Uber and Lyft's point of view. You get paid for time and mileage. The bad part is that time is cheap. Hopefully you will get a tip to make up for it, but no guarantees. My new policy when asked if it is okay to stop for liquor or to go to a drive-thru for food is to ask whether that includes a tip for me. So far, they have not wanted to pay a tip, so they just say, "Forget it." If it's a big trip, I'm more likely to let them request stops, but I mention that I am being paid $6.75/hour to sit and wait, while the cashier checking them out is making $11.50/hour (in San Diego). I ask that they take 5 minutes or less, and we're good. If they want more time, I can drop them there, and they can call for another car when they are done.

Stopping at a Liquor Store (liquor in general)

Liquor has to be closed in a moving vehicle. That is the law. If you get stopped by the police and there is open alcohol in the car, you are in big trouble.

My rule is that all liquor goes in the trunk so that they can't open it before I drop them off. If they want to stop to buy liquor, make them aware of your policy before you stop. If they don't agree to it, offer to end the ride at the liquor store, and they can call for another driver and see how that goes. No single ride is worth it. Even if they rate you 1 star, it is still not worth it. Chances are, if they won't work with you, something worse was likely to happen as well.

Smoking

I have not read this anywhere, but I have a no smoking or vaping policy. You can always say it's company policy, because I am sure that it does not say anywhere that either is permitted while in the vehicle.

Rain and Snow Equal Money

Some people don't like to drive in the rain and snow. The worse the weather, the more potential for money. If it rains, and you meet them with an umbrella, that is a 5 star move.

Boycotts

We all have a different story. Many people think there is a right and wrong thing to do. They will call for a boycott if they think the company is doing something unfair. They likely have a point. But what if you have a family and can't afford to boycott? You should do what you have to do. Your family and kids did not pick your life choices. Do right by them.

Now what if you see someone not boycotting while you are? You have to let them go. You don't know their situation.

I once had a guy approach me at 2 a.m. at a gas station in Las Vegas. I could tell he wasn't right, but he did not look threatening to me, either. He asked me for $10 for gas to get his family home. A lot of people would have turned him away just based on the situation, but I pictured a dad getting out of his car, in front of his wife and kids, to go beg for money. I gave him $100. He took the money, hugged me and went back to his car. I finished pumping my gas, and he was sitting in the driver's seat of his car, rocking and crying. I went over, and he cracked the window so we could talk. I could now see his pregnant wife in the car in the passenger seat. I asked him what was wrong. He said that all he did was ask for the money, and I gave it to him. It was obvious that he needed help and was not getting any, so while my help was small, from my point of view, it was more than he was getting from the rest of the world.

Don't condemn people when you don't know them. Fight for what you believe in, and do what you can do, but never condemn anyone who might just be trying to pay the bills. Maybe they need to drive for Uber or their car will get repossessed. Maybe they need to drive to buy food for their kids. Feel free to talk with them, but make sure you listen. You may be right, but they may be right as well.

Winning is about building up, not tearing down. Just ask Charlie Sheen.

"Never ascribe to malice that which can be explained away by incompetence." - Unknown

Conspiracy Theories

These are things there is no actual evidence for, just circumstantial and anecdotal evidence. And based on that, some theories have evolved. While they make sense, that does not mean they are true - I will even debunk a few for you. Drivers, including myself, have a lot of time to contemplate how they are being taken advantage of, and this book would be incomplete without at least some discussion of a few conspiracy theories that I have encountered.

They Try to Balance Earnings

I have heard that rideshare companies try to balance earnings so that all drivers tend to make about the same amount of money. The freaky thing was, they mentioned the figure of $18/hour, and my rate on Lyft was extremely close to $18/hour at the time. But this amount also includes tips, so that means that if I got more tips, I'd get fewer rides. Is it true? There's no way of knowing. If you are working to raise your hourly rate, and they are working to cap it and not telling you, that is really messed up. One more reason to drive more than one service and switch back and forth.

Uber and Lyft Are Taking Advantage of Their Drivers

Uber and Lyft are companies. Their job is to maximize revenue and minimize costs. Maximizing the income and happiness of their drivers only comes into play when it affects their revenue and costs. For instance, what did Uber and Lyft send you on your birthday? What were the Uber and Lyft Christmas parties like? Answer: They don't do those things. Why? No one high enough up in either organization has figured out that increasing driver happiness would increase revenue at a low enough cost to make it worth it. Until Costco or Southwest start rideshare services, don't expect it to happen.

Are they taking advantage of drivers, passengers, tax law, state and local grants and subsidies? Absolutely, if they are doing their jobs. Just know that and look out for yourself. Be the "independent" in independent contractor.

Uber is Using Mind Games to Keep You on the Road

This turns out to be true. They have people studying driver behavior and ways to get them to drive longer. They have modified their user experience to ping drivers with the next ride before the previous ride is done. You have to internalize this to make good decisions: they don't care about you. And I don't mean that in a mean way. They have, by some estimates, over 1,000,000 drivers. How can they care about each one? They take care of Uber, and you take care of you.

Lyft Is Not Paying for Prime Time Bonus Rides

Honestly, for my first 100 rides, I did not have one ride on Lyft that I could say I got anything but the normal amount on. I don't do the math in my head after each ride, and I have never noticed any signal telling me so. If I am earning more for a trip, they would be well served to create a signal that is more obvious and persistent.

When the forums were claiming that Lyft was fooling us, and that most people had no chance to get this bump, I was a believer. Then came St. Patrick's Day, and the surge fares came flooding in. I averaged a 50% surge for Friday and Saturday. It's still hard to get when there isn't an event, but not impossible.

Lyft Bonus Areas Are Carrots to Get You to Go There

Combine the above with the fact that Lyft bonus areas often last less than the time it takes to put your car in gear, then what do they even mean? I have been sitting in a pink area for 20 minutes, waiting to get a ride, when the pink goes away and I get a call seconds later. I often have pink areas go away as soon as I enter them. Does the software do this to spread the drivers around? It could. Do they do this to keep prices down? They might. Is there any actual evidence of this? Without reading their source code or talking to their programmers, there is no way to know.

It also turns out that the passengers are gaining skills and waiting until surges pass before calling for a ride. That makes it even harder to catch the surge. I have even heard of people on the beach walking out into the ocean and calling for a ride because the ocean wasn't surging. Of course, the driver had no idea where to pick them up.

Lyft Makes the 20% Power Driver Bonus Impossible

Can software say that if you are one ride from the 20% bonus, that you are not assigned any more rides? Absolutely. Do they do it? Who knows? With Lyft I average about 1.2 rides per hour, so if you do the math, you can see how hard it is to get 70 rides in a week. And I only drive the busiest hours, so 70 in a week would likely be over 80 hours in the car. When these things happen to you, it feels like they are doing it on purpose. There is a good chance they are not, but it feels the same either way.

Being at the Pickup Spot is Bad

There is some anecdotal evidence that a driver being at the pickup spot may be worse than being away from the spot. It might be possible that "0 minutes until pickup" might be worse than a "1 minute until pickup" in their software. Do we know? Nope.

Rating the Rating System

There is a difference between critique and criticism. Criticism, like telling someone they are doing poorly is not something you can build on. "You are a bad driver and should be off the road" is useless without some feedback on why the commenter feels that way. Without even any categories of areas to work on, a rating system is mostly useless to the driver, and this applies to both Uber and Lyft.

A critique involves giving feedback as to why you felt a certain rating was warranted. Often the reasons for drivers getting bad ratings are things out of their control. I have read of passengers rating their driver badly because the passenger had requested UberPOOL when they wanted UberX. Or because drivers obeyed the speed limit. Without that context, a 1-4 rating looks like there was something the driver could have done to improve. And by the way, that is an impression the company likes drivers to have. It motivates drivers even though it is a lie.

While the current rating system looks like a grading scale, it is actually is a pass/fail system. The common belief is that you need to keep your score above a 4.6 to guarantee that you will be able to keep driving. To do that requires you get 5 star ratings. If you got all 4 star ratings, you could be deactivated. (On Netflix a 4 star movie is outstanding; on Uber and Lyft, not so much.)

What that means, as I've mentioned before, is that 5 = pass, while 1-4 are degrees of failure. Comparing it to the A-F grading scale we used in school, 5 would be a C, 4 a D, and so forth. There are no A and B equivalents. The scale just stops.

Grading On a Curve

When I was in college, I was graded on a curve. The University of Michigan bragged about bringing in students from the top 1% of students in the country, but at the time, U-M's own grading system was based on how everyone did; that set the scale for what was a "pass" and what was a "fail." An embarrassing part of the equation was that half the students in the class would get a failing grade because, the way the curve was designed, that had to happen. I once got 108 out of 100 (eight out of 10 possible extra credit) and was told that was a C. This is why grading on a curve is useless. If everyone knows the material, they can't all get an A, and if they do, the teacher is fired. Their job, in this situation, is to figure out who's the best and grade them higher.

If you kept up with all that, you realize that the University was just looking for small errors to distinguish between students. They didn't care whether the students understood the material or not. If all the students understood all the material, they fired the instructor because they had no curve on which to grade the students. If the students didn't understand the material, even though the University knew they were top students, they flunked half of them and kept that instructor around.

This is the model Uber and Lyft are using for ratings. Grading on a curve. They assume that over time, the numbers will all be fair and average out to something they can compare with other drivers in your area. That's it. That's the system.

Do they explain the system to passengers? Nope. To drivers? Nope. They rely on ignorance being spread equally in your area. Or at least, in statistician speak, the ignorance gets sampled uniformly by the drivers.

Here is an experiment - Send 10 people into a casino to play one hand of blackjack. Statistically speaking, 4 should win, 1 should tie, and 5 should lose. Now do this for a week. Do they get the same result every night? No. Do they average out over time? They might, but even statisticians acknowledge that there is a thing called a bell curve and outliers.

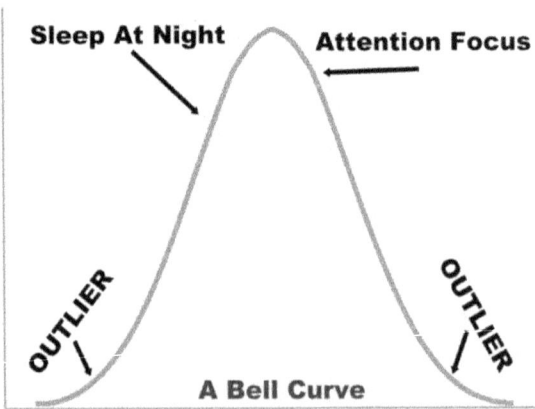

Now send in a million people. Do their numbers more closely match what should happen? Yes. But if you divide the million people into groups of 10, you will have some groups where everyone won and some where everyone lost. This is the difference between statistics and reality. To sleep at night, they just look at the million and say it averages out. But it doesn't. They never average the winnings and losses. Some people just lose.

As a driver, if you want to skew the system in your favor (statistically speaking), explain to passengers (when it makes sense) that 5 = pass and 1-4 equals fail, and that a 4 or less means you should not be driving, because if you got all 4s, you would be deactivated. Also mention that drivers rate passengers as well. I assume that people are less likely to give a bad rating when they know they are getting rated as well. It isn't a one-way street.

Why Stars Don't Work

Amazon uses stars. Netflix uses stars. How can I say they don't work? Because Amazon uses stars, and right next to the rating is a text explanation of why the user gave it that rating. For Netflix, a star rating system works because everyone gets basically the same experience. I mentioned before that I drove a woman from her home to a strip mall and got a 3, but of course, not every driver will drive that woman on the same trip. When I was on the highway driving a van of people for an airport shuttle company, a truck in front of me started dropping bricks in my lane, and they were bouncing all over the road. I was able to switch lanes and get past the truck without running over a brick, getting hit by a brick, or even slowing down on my way to the airport. The people in the van were clapping after they realized they were safe. That is a 5 star ride. Passed. But there's no way to counter the strip mall woman who was on the phone the entire trip. Maybe the only reason she gave me a low rating was because she assumed I would give her a low rating. We'll never know.

Out of my first 42 rated rides for Lyft, the best I can tell is that I got thirty-eight 5 star ratings and four really bad ratings. It made for a 4.8 overall. Why did I get 4 bad ratings? I don't know. Except for one, I don't know which passengers they were. I don't even know if I ever drove the people. I have sometimes gotten pings for people, and when I called them to see where they were, they were 20 miles from where I was told they were. The software still has glitches. Maybe the strip mall woman butt-rated me (similar to butt-dialing) when she put her phone in her pocket. We'll never know.

My Rating System

A rating system is no good unless it's clearly defined and provides feedback. So here goes:

_____ 5 Stars - It was beyond what you would expect from a ride

_____ 4 Stars - Everything was great

_____ 3 Stars - They got me there

_____ 2 Stars - It did not go well. I never want to ride with them again.

_____ 1 Star - Get them off the road ASAP. They are dangerous.

Then, have a comment section for passengers to elaborate on what happened. People need to understand that their rating determines whether you have a job tomorrow. By adding text to the stars, people would understand what their rating meant. Without it, you are relying on the rest of the world to fix your bad design and implementation.

Any rating of 2 or 1 should be appealable by the driver. For instance: "That guy threw up in my car. Here's a picture." If someone throws up in your car, they should not be allowed to rate you. And I would bet that many low ratings are given by people accidentally butt-rating their driver when their phone goes in their pocket. They don't even realize they are being asked a question, and the rating happens as they put away their phone. Uber and Lyft should confirm any rating below 4 with the passenger if they are going to continue to use their current system. I have no idea how anyone would give me less than a 5 star rating, unless they are just trolls (still maintaining a 5 star rating on Uber). I work hard to make sure everything is top of the line, and I only missed one turn in those first 42 trips (coincidentally, it turned out to be a better way to go).

I now have a 5.0 rating on Uber and a 4.94 on Lyft. So this isn't sour grapes.

Were my new rating system to be adopted, Uber or Lyft would start with the lowest-rated drivers and have an anonymous corporate representative take a ride with them. The curve would now be that just the lowest-rated drivers would be required to have a company ride-along. If that didn't go well, or if they did not show up for their ride-along, then they would be deactivated.

After the ride, all ratings by passengers that were lower than the company reps rating would be wiped out, and the driver would be back in the pool. You get three tries to stay out of the bottom. After the third try, you are dropped. The company rep can also recommend that you be dropped after any ride they take with you before that. Basically like the driver's test at the DMV.

This whole mathematically unsound, impersonal, undefined, no-appeal rating system is largely useless. I guarantee you that I could be driving the same car the same way from 11 p.m. to 3 a.m., 5 a.m. to 9 a.m., and 3 p.m. to 7 p.m., and I'd get 3 completely different average ratings for each time period.

On the other end, if a driver gets quite a few ones and twos, they should be brought in to talk about it. Passengers should almost never be giving out ones and twos.

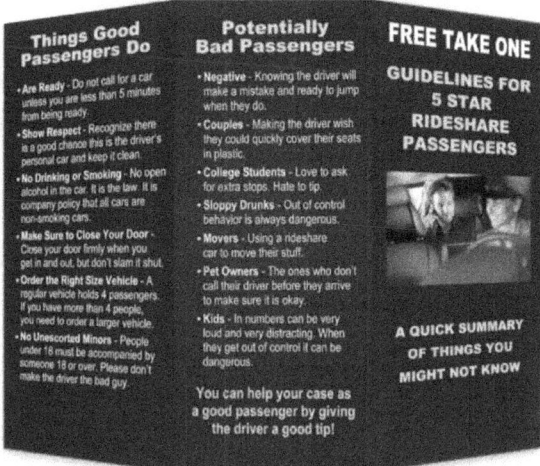

In the Meantime

I made a pamphlet that explains all of this. I'm shocked when passengers who have been using Uber and/or Lyft for years read it and say they had no idea how it worked. They had given 4s before, thinking that was good. Most had given out all 5s, but had no idea what affect their rating was actually having. They were really surprised to find out that the rating system had any effect on a driver's employment. It was like they found out that the gun they had been goofing around with was a real gun, loaded with real bullets.

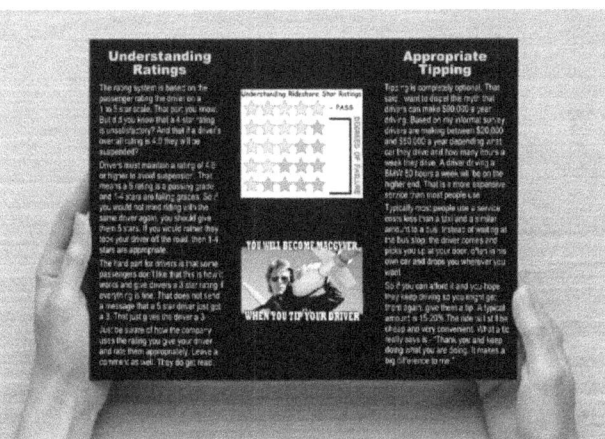

I took those pamphlets and tucked them into the seat pocket facing passengers, so they could read them if they wanted to. It worked exactly as I'd hoped.

"Be so good they can't ignore you." - Steve Martin
What Do I Know?

I am just another driver who, when I was in school, liked to open the back of the book to know the answers before I knew the questions. It always seemed to me that the answers contained the reasons why the questions were important; and they made me curious. Hopefully, with this guide, I have given you some answers and told you why the questions are important. There isn't usually just one good answer to most of the questions, so you need to find the best answers for you.

Why I Wrote the Book

Full disclosure, a big reason I wrote the book was for me. If you want to know a subject well, try and explain it to someone else; if you want to know it on an even deeper level, write down your ideas and let people take shots at them. If you are familiar with open-source code, the power of letting everyone look at it is that they will tell you when you are wrong, and often times, how to improve it. So hopefully this book becomes a match that lights a fire. If all goes well, there will be a second edition that updates everything. Keep those cards and letters coming.

Top 4 Things to Keep in Mind

If you get nothing else out of this book, make sure you do these four things well:

- Be positive. Everyone wants to be a part of a success.

- Be confident. When you do your best, there is no more.

- Be clean. It gives the passengers confidence that they are in good hands.

- Be a good driver. Your job is to get everyone there safely.

With that as your base, you can go far.

About Me

In this guide, I've talked about my personal experiences a bit, but I'll confess that I was hesitant to. I didn't want you to think I'd figured everything out from the start and have people just mimic what I did. For instance, I'm a person who bought a new car to rideshare drive. A really bad idea in general. I did it because I needed to buy a car, since that was the whole point, and my sister worked at Ford, so I could get a good deal; plus, the new hybrids had size, great gas mileage, and financial incentives. But that was me. Use all that information to understand the process, not as an endorsement of what you should do.

I live in San Diego, California, and I am a computer game developer. My company is Game Mechanics, and I have games on Steam and Amazon.

Our one car is a 2011 Mazda 6. I bought a 2017 Ford C-Max Hybrid with black exterior and interior. It gets 40 MPG.

I have worked a lot of jobs: ice cream scooper, bus boy, pizza delivery man, airport shuttle driver, hospital orderly, medical software developer, and game software developer. I have two award winning short films on "Funny or Die," and I played on a semi-pro soccer team - once in the 70,000-seat Pontiac Silverdome. I have written and produced TV commercials (that have aired on TV), and I have saved companies, only to be laid off less than a month later. All those different things happened over time. There was no straight path. I always tried to do the best thing at every time in my life. Today I am writing this book.

Now let's focus on you.

What Does All This Say to You?

At every point in my life, there has always been someone who was sure they knew a better way for me. But don't let anyone's criticism of you affect you. Let them rain, and you be the parade. If your plan was to sit on the couch and let everyone else pay your bills, that is one thing. But if you are out there fighting to do the right thing, I am behind you 100%. You bought this book and read this far. You obviously want to be better. So ignore the noise and get out there.

Time is the most precious resource we have. Don't let other people take it away from you or tell you how to spend it. And don't waste others' time, either. Honestly, everything else is a distraction.

The Big Sendoff

Knowledge and discipline win the game. Knowing what to do and then doing it. There are a lot of little suggestions in this book to help you be prepared for the battles that will come to you. Do your best. Nobody can ask for more. You can't always win, but you can always try. Now try smarter.